The Untold Tales of a Sailor at Sea

The Untold Tales of a Sailor at Sea

Author L.C. Tang
Illustrator Oscar David

XULON PRESS ELITE

Xulon Press Elite
2301 Lucien Way #415
Maitland, FL 32751
407.339.4217
www.xulonpress.com

Exulon
ELITE

Printed in the United States of America.

ISBN-13: 978-1-6322-1427-0

To all seafarers and passengers cruising at sea

Contents

Prologue

The opportunity to board an airplane and leave the country is always considered a privilege in my mind. I never had the desire to travel outside of my community as my whole world revolved around a few square kilometers within my city. I was quite content.

But then, I realize I have a wonderful dream and I go.

My journey at sea spans over a decade, from starting as a passenger sailing on various cruise lines. Witnessing the exciting life of the crew members onboard piqued my interest enough to embrace a life at sea, and I wholeheartedly welcomed the invitation.

My dream is now my reality. I have explored over 140 ports of call, traveled to over seventy-five countries, and entertained people from all walks of life for over thirty years.

I wake up and climb off my bed to look out the window and realize my window is not the port hole I long to experience again. All I see is a concrete jungle of buildings in a city rather than the calm waves of the ocean from the cabin of a cruise ship.

The excitement and adventures of being at sea drive me to start packing as I am ready to sail again.

Chapter 1
Happy Birthday

*Twenty years from now you will be more disappointed by
the things that you didn't do than by the ones you did do.
So throw off the bowlines. Sail away from the safe harbour.
Catch the trade winds in your sails. Explore.
Dream. Discover. Mark Twain*

It is a beautiful, warm, May spring day as I carry my luggage and joining papers, with passport in hand, up the gangway. I am to begin my sojourn as a crew member on my very first contract onboard a luxury cruise ship. I am thrilled to be joining as a member of the Entertainment Department, and I am still in awe as I gaze at this giant, eighteen-story-tall luxury cruise ship. I realize I am finally living my dream job. This is another birthday present to myself coming to fruition. My heart palpitates with excitement as my hands sweat with nervousness trying to keep a grip on my heavy luggage. My mind is absorbed in imagining what is to unfold for the coming weeks of my first experience of life at sea.

A few months leading up to my thirtieth birthday, I was finally settled into a new apartment and career. I asked my girlfriends what they had planned for their milestone thirtieth birthdays. I was living the mundane life of routine, had finally paid off my heavy student loans, was out of a toxic relationship, and finally felt free to start a new chapter. I was eager to find ways to celebrate my upcoming birthday. I decided to do some research and exercise some financial foresight for my upcoming milestone. I asked around, discovering what many people did to memorialize their big birthdays. One girlfriend said she lived at home until she saved up enough money to buy herself a new car upon turning thirty since that was her dream. Another girlfriend told me she would buy herself many diamonds for her hand as she thought she never would find a man to grace her with enough diamonds in her future marriage. Yet another girlfriend told me she took her first trip to New York City and blew all her money partying for her big milestone.

After months of surveying the people around me, I concluded I wanted an adventure that would provide lifetime memories and usher me into a new chapter. I really did not want anything materialistic; I just wanted to make some meaningful memories. One day as I walked home from work, it dawned on me that I should take a cruise all by myself and make some happy remembrances far away at sea where nobody knew me. A small part of me wanted to escape my life here on land—the trials, tribulations, traumas, and bad relationship that led me to this point.

I was excited at the idea of doing something adventurous all by myself, so after work I went straight to the travel agency and purchased a single ticket for a Caribbean cruise. Being a solo traveler for the first time outside of the country, I learned very quickly that single supplement charges run up the bill very quickly. After a week in the Caribbean, I came home to open my credit card statement and see an astonishing $6,000.00 expenditure for only seven days at sea! I was back in financial debt. I could not believe I had put myself back in that situation after six years of paying off my large educational loans and moving expenses. I was utterly dismayed as I looked at my bill. Shaking my head, I thought to myself, "I don't even drink alcohol. How is this total even possible?" After a few moments of shock, while still holding the bill, I immediately decided that I would not pay again for having fun at sea. I got the brilliant idea that I wanted to be a part of the adventure and excitement of working at sea. My determined hunt for an escape on the ocean started that day. Now, eight months later, here I am walking up to the immigration checkpoint at the airport armed with my cruise line joining papers, passport, and a one-way ticket to an American state to join the ship.

I am pulled aside for interrogation into Room B. I panic as my heart starts to race. The officer asks why I only have a one-way ticket, followed by countless questions. I slide across the table my joining papers and explain that as a crew member I am only given a one-way airplane ticket because I must finish my contract and complete my duties in order to be given a return ticket home. The immigration officer picks up the telephone and asks me to leave the office. As I sit anxiously alone in the waiting room, I continually look at my watch and think, "I do not want to miss my flight!" If the officer refuses my papers, I will be stuck forever on land to live a boring life of routine, teaching clients at the community gym. I am lost in my thoughts when the door opens, and the officer comes out. "I called your company; you are good to go. Have a great contract," he says in a stern voice as he hands me back my papers. I am so relieved. Finally, my adventure at sea can start!

After walking up the steep, inclined plane to the top of the gangway, I pull up to the security guard and show my joining card. I follow the other joining crew members and place my luggage on the conveyor belt for security screening and walk through the metal detector without a hitch. The first two weeks on this luxury cruise liner is a whirlwind to say the least. I work in various roles that change every day within the Entertainment Department. I have a lot to learn and many on-board training sessions to attend. I am like a deer caught in headlights every day. My mind is swimming to grasp the sailors' colloquial lingo that is new to me, and every day I try to navigate through the labyrinth of corridors, feeling like a rat in a maze.

Throughout my entire contract, my thoughts often go back to the movie *Titanic* I saw in early 1998. I also frequently reflected upon my past as it has been since I left my toxic relationship. I now realize I have somewhat recovered and survived physically, emotionally, and mentally from that abusive situation. With much determination, I currently focus on my intent to make new memories living this new chapter of my life. Every day I experience long and demanding days at sea, but the work ethic required is nothing new for me. Each day I start at 7:00 a.m. and get to bed just after midnight with only a few short breaks to eat meals in between shifts. With the passing days, I slowly learn that a demanding long day of work coupled with constant noise, assaults on one's senses, and basic life deprivations over an extended period will challenge any soul at sea, whether sailing as a passenger or a crew member.

Many times, after my shift, I get lost trying to find my cabin. Working at the back of the ship, called the stern, and navigating through crew corridors behind camouflaged doors in order to get to the front of the ship, called the bow, is a feat. Tonight, I am scheduled to work till 1:00 a.m. and I am alone. Finishing my shift, I start my 600-feet journey back to the bow of the ship from the stern. At this time of night, most crew members have already finished their duties and are at the Crew Bar hanging out in the open-spaced lounge with other crew members, dancing, partying, and relaxing with drinks and cigarettes. There are not many crew members around the rest of the ship for me to ask for directions. Unfortunately, I am lost again trying to find my cabin. The majority of cabins for crew members are located several decks below from the passengers quarters and are numbered differently than the passenger cabins, and there are so many watertight doors in each zone along the way in the bowels of the ship.

Early this morning, the Captain had announced to the crew that we were headed into rough seas, and that meant in the evening all watertight doors would be closed. I did not think much of the announcement until this very moment as I navigate my way. I am now on Deck Three below the water line, and as my feet land on the bottom of the flight of stairs, I see a closed watertight door in front of me. It is a dead-end. Immediately, the scene from the *Titanic* comes flooding back into my mind. How do I get to my cabin? It is 1:20 a.m. and I want to sleep. I am so tired, and I must get up to work in less than eight hours. I walk back up the flight of stairs and try to find another that leads to Deck Three. I end up on the starboard side where the cabin numbers are labeled with odd numbers. After turning left, right, right, left, right, I lose my sense of direction. At every turn, I come up to a watertight door and I cannot get to my cabin, which is an even numbered cabin. Having an even numbered cabin means I need to get to the portside of the ship. I am stuck on the starboard side, meaning I am on the right side of the ship.

For the life of me, I cannot figure out how to get out of this maze. A frantic feeling drains me as I look at my watch.

It is now 1:45 a.m. and I feel trapped in a maze. I feel so helpless; all the crew corridors are quiet with sleeping crew members and there is no one around to ask for directions. I feel tired, lost, and alone, and the little girl inside me just wants to cry. I know crying will not solve my problem, so I tell myself to buck up and correct the situation. I think to myself, "There isn't a crybaby in this thirty-year-old woman!" I have cried enough in the previous chapter of my life. I am determined. "God help me!" I cry out loud in frustration as I navigate towards the exit sign.

I finally find a flight of stairs leading up to Deck Four and I climb them in the hope of finding another crew member for help. I walk up and down the main crew corridor. The main corridor stretches the entire length of the ship, just one deck below the passengers' quarters; is called the i95. It stretches from the bow to stern, all 804 feet. Not one single person is in sight. However, my watch reads 1:55 a.m. and I do not know what else to do, so I cry out to God, "Help me, Lord. I need help. Please send someone to help me."

Squinting down the long i95 corridor on Deck Four I see an officer in white with stripes on his shoulders about 300 feet ahead heading my way. "Excuse me, sir, could you please help me?" I ask sheepishly in quiet desperation. His kind eyes and soft voice soothe me, and he replies, "What can I do for you?"

"I want to go home, and I cannot find my cabin. Please help me, I want to go home and sleep," I plead.

He smiles and replies, "You must be a new joiner and are lost." His eyes move to my name badge over my left breast.

"Well, hello Lincee. What is your cabin number?" I do not even remember to look at his name badge which lists his name, his country, position, and rank. I just want help to get to my cabin. The kind officer walks me to my cabin as I share with him my frustrating journey since my shift finished at 1:00 a.m. He explains to me how the cabins and watertight doors are laid out in the maze. My mind tries to focus on his words, but I all want to do is take a hot shower, brush my teeth, and sleep under my warm blanket in my cold cabin under the waterline. I forget all he says to me; I just thank him.

I finally get to the top bunk of my bed and try to fall asleep, shivering under my blanket as I listen to the waves splashing against the other side of my cabin wall. The sway of the ship creaks with every swell of the ocean on the other side of my bunk. A cold, chilly air fills my cabin and, even with my blankets up to my chin, there is no relief as I drift off to sleep.

The next day, I work a long day entertaining the passengers all over the ship in different stations, and again I am the last one in my department to lock up. Unfortunately, I find myself in the exact same situation as last night, heading towards the bow in hopes of locating my cabin. I feel like a little kid trying to find my house on the street, yet I cannot remember how to walk home. I try desperately to recall the officer's directions and explanation from the night before about the watertight doors, but I cannot even remember his name. All his words and directions are floating mixed up in my mind as I search every corridor and flights of stairs in hope they lead to my cabin. I look at my watch and I know my roommate is already sound asleep, so I cannot even dare call the cabin to wake her up and ask her to come pick me up on the i95.

It is already 1:20 a.m. as I stand in the corridor trying to decipher the map of the crew corridors. An officer comes walking down the i95. As he approaches me, he interrupts my thoughts and smiles as he walks towards me. Suddenly, I remember the officer who helped me last night is named Michael, but this officer is not tall with blonde hair as he is. This officer is shorter and has brown hair, but he smiles at me and says "Hello!" to which I am shocked.

I learned very quickly about rank at sea. Officers of higher rank generally do not talk with crew of lower rank unless they are in the same department or a crew member's direct supervisor. I look at his name badge and learn he is a Bridge Officer of second rank. I guess the lost look on my face makes him cheerfully ask me the question, "Well, hello, Lincee. Are you lost?" His eyes move from my face to my name badge then back to my eyes.

I reply in dismay, "Yes, I am lost AGAIN!" with a bit of embarrassment.

"Let me help you. What is your cabin number?" he replies in his thick Croatian accent.

I suddenly feel relieved and answer his question to which he replies, "Why don't I show you a shortcut to your cabin and give you a quick tour, too, since you are a new joiner?"

I feel tired but relieved that perhaps I just made a friend. Making friends at sea is a bit hard for me since I am a quiet introvert and often spend time observing my surroundings. I am not quite the social butterfly at sea like I am on land. Back home in North America, I am an extrovert. On land, I am the gym instructor, confident in my element, personally training clients to reach their fitness goals. Yet here at sea, I am new. I feel lost and out of my element trying to build a new life and identity for myself. A hint of trepidation and shyness lies within me when it comes to dealing with ranks and positions depicted by colours of uniform.

I follow beside the handsome Croatian Bridge Officer and we chat as he takes me up to the top deck at the stern of the ship. As we walk up another flight of stairs in the passenger corridor at the back of the ship, I tell him, "My cabin is on Deck Three at the front of the ship. My cabin is in Zone One, not Zone Five at the back of the ship." Even though I often get lost and lose orientation, I know we are going in the opposite direction, far from my cabin. He reassures me that he is showing me a shortcut from where I originally started as he opens many camouflaged doors labeled for crew. He keeps looking at the ceiling and the tiny labels on each door. I do not think much of it; I just follow him for this tour of the ship. There is no other crew around at the back of the ship at this time of night.

Each door labeled "crew only" has a tiny marker with numbers and code words on the top corner unbeknownst to many passing passengers. Behind many of these crew area doors and corridors, there are no cameras. Cameras are generally only placed on the ceiling in passenger public areas. The officer and I are now at the back of the ship and it is already 1:30 a.m. We can only hear the propellers and engines below, pushing the cruise ship forward. I can hear the wake of water splashing behind the ship as it sails along the cold, Alaskan waters.

He finally finds a door labeled for crew that opens to a flight of stairs heading down; there are no cameras in sight. I step over the ridge and the heavy door slams behind me. I am relieved to be out of the Alaskan cold air. Behind the heavy steel door, I no longer hear the wake of the water nor its splash against the ship though I can still feel the engine shake the entire back of the ship beneath our feet.

Suddenly, this Croatian Officer pushes me against the wall at the top of the stairs, grabs my wrist, and holds it against the wall. With his other hand, he very quickly rips the zipper on my uniform and pulls my panties down. His heavy body pushes up against me as he unzips his own white officer trousers. I can feel his hard penis pressing against me. I push him away with terror in my voice and eyes. I yelp, "Stop, stop, NO, NO! What are you doing? Please stop!"

No one is around, and no one would be able hear my shouts for help even if I screamed at the top of my lungs. I feel so helpless. This officer wants his way with me, and I cannot believe I thought he genuinely was helping me with a short cut tour to my cabin. His hand glides down from my wrist and grabs a fistful of my left breast. He squeezes so hard that it hurts. I keep shouting "NO, NO, please stop!" as I fight back. His strong body holds me up against the wall. I am terrified. With all I have, I push and fight back.

I left a life of abuse and violence back home, and on this ship all I wanted was to start a new chapter and make new memories. From all those years at the gym, training, lifting weights, and pumping iron, I am built solid with cut muscles. I am not about to let myself be raped! I fight back with anger in my voice and blurt out forcefully as I push his face away from my lips, "Why? Why? You said you would help me, give me a tour and shortcut!" Keeping his body still up against mine, he replies as I push his hands away from between my legs, "I gave you a tour, now it's my turn to tour your body!" His voice is full of angry lust, dripping with a sailor's hunger for sex.

"Lincee, I want you. I want you now! I need to feel you! I want you so bad!" the officer continues, breathing heavily against me. I can feel his penis hard up against me as I push him away again. He quickly and forcefully grabs my hand, and down the flight of stairs I am thrown.

The only way a crew member can get the release he needs without being caught is to put another crew member to silence. Putting a crime to silence means throwing the victim overboard at the back of the ship where no cameras are running, and no screams can be heard above the loud engine and the propellers chopping up the water. This is the best option for those guilty as no accountability is necessary for committing a crime at sea. The propellers will suck the body under the ship and chop up any evidence that a crime has been committed. No one would suspect anything happened if I were silenced as such. To throw a fellow crew member or passenger overboard would silence any story, leaving the perpetrator free to walk innocently.

Being the strong weightlifting instructor that I am, this officer quickly realizes he will not be able to throw me overboard if I am conscious and fighting back. I certainly do not want to be fish food for Alaskan salmon. The officer quickly learns he cannot fight my strength, but he still wants my body badly. He remains a threat every day going forward.

Later I learn that the officer who helped me find my cabin the first night works in the same department on the Bridge as this hurtful Croatian Officer. Officer Michael had told the other Bridge Officers that there was a new joiner named Lincee and she had gotten lost finding her cabin. This bit of information gave the Croatian Officer an idea to seek me out after my shift. My name had spread like wildfire since my coming aboard a few days ago. I am fresh meat. I quickly learn there are only twenty-three women working onboard and 670 men on this ship. The ratio is astounding. Every sailor is sexually frustrated at sea, working for months on end deprived of the comforts and physical gratifications that can ease the long, hard workdays that continue for months on end. Every woman on the ship has their choice of selecting a boyfriend from an eager pool of sex-starved sailors. Even the cheap access to endless alcohol and cigarettes is not enough to satiate the sexual appetite of a sailor at sea.

The sailors on this ship are comprised of approximately eighty percent from the Philippines, ten percent from India, and a small handful of Americans and Canadians in the Entertainment Department. The other approximate eight percent are from Europe, and all the Bridge Officers are European or from the British Isles. Since I am new to the life in this industry, I am unaware I was looked upon as fresh meat the moment I stepped on the gangway; the sailors had their lusting eyes on this unsuspecting crew member. It is a game of cat and mouse and little did I know I would be a target each day.

Chapter 2
Food for Thought

The pessimist complains about the wind; the optimist
expects it to change; the realist adjusts the sails.
William Arthur Ward

It is a glorious sunny day at sea as the ship sails up the coast of British Columbia heading into the Alaskan inlets. The calm waves give us smooth sailing and the cool waters are kind to the hull of the ship. It is another exciting day at sea for the passengers. The Captain's voice comes over the ship at twelve noon every day announcing the weather report and navigational update. Although the announcement is meant for the passengers, it also is a quiet reminder for the crew that lunch is being served in the eating quarters on the crew deck, known as the "mess", located just one deck below the passenger quarters and below the water line. Every day at twelve noon, crew members scurry down to the mess to get a taste of what is being dished out of the heating pans in the cafeteria buffet line, each aiming to grab the best morsel before all of them are taken.

Crew members are categorized generally into one of three ranks at sea which dictates uniform, privileges, eating, and sleeping quarters. Entertainers are considered crew in the middle rank, referred to as "staff rank", sandwiched between officers dressed in white who are the highest rank and everyone else who fall into the lowest rank. This last group is simply referred to as "crew" and has the most limited privileges onboard.

The food for the officers is served in the Officer Mess and is the same high-quality food enjoyed by the passengers; it is even the same dinner menu. The ranks of staff and crew each have a separate dining area and the food is laid out buffet-style in an atmosphere much like a high school cafeteria. On the ship I am sailing, due to its smaller size, members of the staff rank have the same food privileges as officers despite our dining in separate rooms, but we get to order only two items on the passenger menu at lunch and dinner. In the Officer Mess, the tables have tablecloths and the officers are served like they are dining in a restaurant, including hot beverages like coffee and tea served with dessert. There are no tablecloths and no hot beverages in the Staff and Crew Messes. In the Staff Mess, only a pitcher of water dripping with condensation sits at the center of the table on a plate and we must collect our own cutlery. In the Crew Mess, everything is self-serve, including the beverages which come from a dispenser like at a McDonald's, and everyone is required to collect his or her own cutlery and napkins prior to sitting down at a table with their tray of food.

Today I am running late after my morning shift and arrive at the Staff Mess shortly after noon to find that all the seats are taken. Much like the stereotypical high school mentality, certain tables are reserved for the cool kids and certain tables are reserved for certain departments. Generally, the musicians sit with other musicians, the Production Department sits with its own, the dancers sit with their troupe, and so on, so when I arrive late, I know there is a seat reserved for me with my team at my regular table. I walk over and place my uniform crew jacket over the empty chair. Everyone has already placed their lunch order.

I walk up to the crew member standing by the order counter who I think is taking today's lunch orders. I cheerfully greet the crew member; "Hello, I would like to place my order for lunch, please." I do not even look at the colour of his uniform, not noticing that crew members working in the Food and Beverage Department only wear white uniforms with a vest whether they serve passengers or crew. I am still considered a new joiner after being onboard for only two weeks, so this crew member looks surprisingly at me, slowly reaches over to the pad of paper on the counter, and precisely asks, "What is your order, Lincee?" while looking at my name badge.

"One cheeseburger with fries, please." I smile in return, then turn to walk back to my table, but he continues, "Excuse me, Miss Lincee, cabin number, please?"

I turn around puzzled. "Excuse me, you need my cabin number?" I am bewildered he has asked for it since this has never been requested before. I think to myself, perhaps the ship charges us crew for the food we eat and on Fridays they need our cabin number to send the bill. I am confused, so I quietly tell him my cabin number and watch him write it on the pad of paper beside my order. I do not think much of it, so I figure it must be legitimate. I walk back to the table and sit quietly thinking, mentally trying to calculate how much my lunch bill will be after only being onboard for two weeks and if the bill must be tallied up on the last Friday of the month. I do not recall seeing any prices on the crew menu, so I cannot figure out what just happened and how to tally the costs.

My silence and the bewildered look on my face catches the attention of my colleagues. My roommate, Katerina, who also works in my department, pipes up in her Mexican accent, "What's the matter, Lincee? You have a funny look on your face. What's up?"

I lean over and ask Katerina, "When do we get the bill to pay for the food we eat?" Suddenly the entire table goes silent and everyone's wide eyes are on me. I take in everyone's shocked silence and eagerly await the answer to my question.

Katerina replies, "What do you mean 'when do we get a bill?' The food is free, Lincee. Don't you know? It's been two weeks that you have been onboard and there hasn't been a bill yet."

Perplexed, I reply back, "It's the end of the month, don't we get a bill? I didn't see the prices on the menu for the food we ordered."

My supervisor Peter turns to me and says, "Lincee, where in the world did you get the idea that we have to pay for the food we eat? We are crew; food is included in our contract."

I go on to explain my confusion, "Well, the guy just asked me for my cabin number and wrote it down beside my cheeseburger order, so isn't he going to submit it and I get the bill at some point?"

At this point, the entire table bursts out laughing at me. Katerina patiently asks, "Lincee, who did you give our cabin number to? You NEVER give your cabin number to anyone; our phone will ring off the hook!"

Peter chimes in, "Did you place your lunch order with that guy?" as he points to the crew member in the white uniform and vest at the order counter.

I answer back, "I don't recall, Peter. I didn't pay attention to which crew member I spoke with or the colour of his uniform."

Peter continues and points, questioning me with wide eyes of laughter, "Look over there, Lincee. There is a guy in a green jumper by the counter too. He is the electrician fixing the light switch, did you give *him* your lunch order?"

The manager of my department is sitting at the table with us. Despite being of officer rank, she sits and eats lunch with the rest of us in the Staff Mess. She bursts out laughing at me while shaking her head. "Lincee, you need to pay attention to whom you are talking to. Look at the name on the badge. It has their job title and you don't place your lunch order with the electrician. You will never get your lunch!" The entire table of fellow crew members are in stitches laughing hysterically and loudly. They are laughing so hard at me they are clutching their stomachs as tears run down their faces. Even my roommate, Katerina, is laughing and shaking her head at me. Both my manager and my supervisor, Peter, are laughing at me. My face is beet red from embarrassment as every table in the mess has crew members looking at our table, wondering why everyone is laughing but me with my look of complete humiliation.

Minutes pass and everyone's lunch order arrives. Except mine. I wait patiently for my cheeseburger to arrive thinking that since I arrived late and placed my order late, my lunch will be late. Ten minutes pass and I am getting hungry and the lunch hour is almost over. I need to have enough time to eat, get to my cabin, brush my teeth, freshen up, and then navigate the maze to get back up to the top deck in time for my shift. I kindly ask the crew member in white, who I now know is the waiter, "Excuse me sir, do you know when my lunch order will arrive?"

"Miss Lincee, you didn't place an order with me today. I saw you sitting with your team and you did not come up to me, so I thought you were not hungry. I do not have your order."

The entire table bursts out laughing at me again. It is poor Lincee today as I do not have lunch because I gave my order to the electrician in the green jumper instead of this crew member in the white uniform. I am hungry despite stuffing my face with the bread on the table and now I do not have time to order lunch. Lesson learned! Always read the name badge of the crew member you are talking with. Suddenly, the image of the Croatian Officer who "helped" me the other day to find my cabin comes flooding back. I do not know his name, but I remember his face.

The ship finally docks in the port of Juneau around 3:00 p.m., and the crew will be permitted ashore after all the passengers have disembarked to explore another Alaskan port and enjoy their pre-arranged tours. About an hour and a half after docking, the Captain finally announces that crew shore leave is granted. It is a mass exodus of crew getting off the ship. I do not feel very good with an empty stomach and the bad experience with the Croatian Officer the other night. I want to be alone and rest. I tell my roommate, Katerina, to go ashore as I want to stay onboard. Katerina tells me, "Come Lincee, we can go to McDonald's and you can get your cheeseburger in Juneau. Some fresh air will be good for you."

I quietly agree and get out of my uniform into my civilian clothes. I feel much better in the comfort of my own clothes as I walk across the gangway with Katerina into the Port of Juneau, easily blending in with local tourists

and other passengers. Once in town, Katerina wants to go to the public library for use of the computers and free Wi-Fi. I want my cheeseburger, so we go our separate ways. I climb up the hill to McDonald's and order my meal. I find a quiet table in the corner and finish my late afternoon lunch. I feel a bit better now that my stomach is no longer growling with hunger. I step outside to the phone booth by the McDonald's entrance to call home. I cannot afford a cell phone on my salary and it is much easier to call collect or use a phone card.

I call my sister and tell her, with tears running down my face, everything that has transpired since I was interrogated at the airport to every trivial challenge I have experienced since I joined he ship. I purposely leave out the part about the Croatian Officer. I cry and cry over the telephone, and my sister can hear the pain and broken spirit in my voice. After I hang up, I call my mother as I do not want her to worry about me. I conjure up a strong voice and story to tell her I am doing fine and enjoying my time in Alaska. Then I use the remaining time on my phone card to call and check my voice messages on my answering machine. The phone card only lasts thirty minutes at $10 USD. Phone calls are expensive, and phone cards are such a commodity for crew at sea. Later I would learn that amongst the crew members one can trade a phone card for a sexual favour. I know I can always call my sister and mom collect if I need and will not have to resort to begging around for a calling card if the vending machines are empty.

As I slowly walk back towards the ship, I find a green bench along the pier that faces out toward the water. It is a quiet nook behind the hustle and bustle of a large souvenir shop. I decide to sit down for a moment to enjoy this new-found solitude away from crew and passengers. I am finally alone with my thoughts as I lean back against the bench cross-legged and stare at the snow-capped mountain peaks on this chilly day.

Slowly and deeply I breathe in the fresh, crisp Alaskan air while sitting alone. As I exhale, I cry out, "Oh God, do you hear me? Help me! I am broken, I am hurt, I need you!" Tears run down my face for quite some time as I sit still looking out over the cold water. I am at a loss for words. My heart and body aches. I need some comfort. I need a lending ear, a warm heart, a friend, my soul aches for some peace. With tears still streaming down my cheeks, I do not know how I will finish this contract. A part of me wants to go home, back to North America, where I feel safe in my mundane routine in my small downtown apartment where everything is familiar. I want to be strong, I want to start a new chapter, I want revenge, I want karma to take place, I want vindication. I think, most of all, I just want to be loved, respected, and cherished and not looked upon as a fresh piece of meat. How can I go back on that ship and face the Croatian Officer when our paths cross again? Continuing to cry my heart out, I ask God with an urgency in my voice, "Help me, God! Give me wisdom! Speak to me please!" After a few moments pass, I feel the Holy Spirit fill me as I sit alone on the bench and scripture comes to mind:

"Peace I leave with you; my peace I give you. I do not give to you as the world gives. Do not let your heart be troubled and do not be afraid" (John 14:27 NIV).

All those years attending Sunday school while growing up planted seeds deep in my heart. Now a sense of peace fills me as this Scripture, held deep within me, comes flooding forward. Today I desperately need the harvest of such seeds and the words of comfort I receive when I cried out to God.

I hold my head up and wipe my tears as I walk with confidence back onto the ship to complete the rest of my contract, come whatever may across my path. Despite having faced all the vicissitudes, setbacks, and struggles up to this point on land and at sea, my heart is filled with a faith of resilience and fortitude to forge ahead.

When I return to the ship, it is only 5:00 p.m., so I still have some time before my evening shift. I change into my uniform as is required when in passenger areas. I find the chapel located midship and go inside to pray. I play some piano music in hopes of lifting my spirit. I crave some quiet time to practice and play some uplifting church hymns.

On a port day, the passengers are all ashore as are most crew members. Nobody likes to be on board the ship on a port day unless they absolutely must be, such as when assigned In-Port-Manning duties, also known as IPM. Yet I came back early and find solace in the chapel alone with my thoughts and piano playing. I always feel comfort at the piano whether I am practicing my scales for warm-up, perfecting a prelude by Bach or a sonata by Mozart, or just improvising. Soon my fingers find some worship songs to play and I am singing praises alone in the chapel. Suddenly, I hear the door swing open and in walks an officer in white. I freeze and stop playing. It is Michael, the officer who helped me the first day find my cabin. My shoulders relax a bit, but I know I may be in trouble for playing the piano without permission or in trouble for not checking the schedule of the chapel.

Michael walks in with a smile. "Hello, Lincee, I heard someone playing the piano as I walked by. Please don't stop playing, it sounds so beautiful." He stands at the entrance of the chapel, then closes the door behind him and finds a seat. He sits down, turns toward me, and urges me to continue playing. "Please, Lincee, don't stop. I did not know you played the piano or even sing. You have such a beautiful voice."

Suddenly, I feel so nervous. I put my hands on my lap and turn to him. "Michael," I pause and then continue, "I am born a pianist. I am a musician."

Michael kindly replies, "You are a musician? Yet you are not wearing the uniform of a musician. You are wearing another uniform for the Entertainment Department." Michael remembered I had been wearing a different uniform the previous night when he helped me. Now I am wearing another type of uniform that anyone within the Entertainment Department could wear. Michael is perplexed at the change in my work clothes. I go on to explain,

"I played the piano last night in the lounge after my other shift. I did double duty last night with two uniforms."

Michael and I exchange pleasantries, and I begin to feel comfortable being alone with him though I look up at the ceiling and surreptitiously count the hidden cameras. Michael notices me looking up at the ceiling scanning and counting the cameras. I feel relieved there are closed-circuit cameras in this passenger area so if anything should happen, I will have recorded evidence. In that moment, my mind flashes back to the other officer who attacked me.

Michael interrupts my thoughts and comes over to the piano and sits on the bench beside me. He is so kind and soft-spoken toward me as we chat. He tells me that he took piano lessons as a kid back home in England and never continued as he grew up because he did not have discipline. He puts his hand on the keys and tries to play a piece with much embarrassment. Michael is nothing like the Croatian Officer from the Bridge. Michael asks me for some piano lessons. My heart softens for this man as I let my guard down. Perhaps today I made a friend. This afternoon we start the first of many piano lessons in this chapel. It is a fortuitous coincidence that we met at this location which begins our friendship because of my love of music.

As days pass, with each chance and break I have, I go to the chapel and practice the piano so I can perform flawlessly and with confidence for the passengers. I play in the lounges for the intoxicated late-night crowds. Sometimes my heart leads me to sing along with my tunes. Tonight, after my shift, I go straight to my cabin below deck to change into my other formal uniform. With music folder in tow under my arm and bottle of water in the other, I go up to the top deck to perform the piano at the back of the ship. I see fellow crew members from the Entertainment Department in the crowd eating pizza at the tables. They cheer me on as I play and belt out tunes. Passengers make some requests for certain songs and one passenger even comes up to sing alongside the piano as my fingers grace the keys. The musician in me feels such satisfaction and my mind is finally satiated.

It is about 1:30 a.m. and the crowd thins out and the crew slowly disappear. I continue to play the piano as the remaining crew clean up the dining room, and when I see the cleaning staff pull out the vacuum, I know it is almost 2:00 a.m. My shift is finished so I get up and start to head toward my cabin on the other end of the ship. There are no other crew members in sight as I walk towards the elevator. I cannot stop smiling as I carry my music folder under my arm, and I feel such elation after entertaining the passengers and crew with my love of music. As I get off the elevator and turn the corner, suddenly, out of nowhere, the Croatian Officer comes up beside me and walks with me. I am in such a state of surprise; I feel terrified, but I try not to show it as I pick up my pace.

"I heard you sing tonight, and I heard you play the piano in the lounge. You played the piano; now I want to play you,

Lincee. I want to make you sing for me." He speaks calmly in his thick accent.

I pick up my pace and look around for another crew member, but no one is in sight. It is 2:00 a.m. and no passengers are around either. I do not say anything as the smile on my face leaves me for terse lips and a quickened pace. The Croatian Officer keeps walking beside me. My heart is pounding with fear as we walk silently in the passenger areas. I keep looking at the ceiling for the hidden closed-circuit cameras. I know he will not attack or touch me in the public passenger areas where the cameras are active. As I head toward my cabin, I think to myself perhaps he remembers my cabin number from the other night when I gave it to him thinking he would help me find it. I sincerely hope he does not remember where I live. As we pass by the crew door on Deck Five that leads to the pizzeria, he grabs me and shoves me hard through the heavy steel door that leads inside the pizzeria kitchen. I am in such shock from the heavy shove against the door that I drop my music folder on the floor.

As I bend over to pick up my music folder, he shoves me hard against the pizzeria counter where I bang my head. I feel dizzy, and suddenly I feel his hands on me. He rips open my uniform blouse while his hand reaches beneath my uniform skirt and yanks my panties down. I hear a rip as he shoves his hand between my legs and tears the panties off. He pushes me hard up against the cold metal counter. I feel dizzy as I look up at the ceiling and notice there are no cameras in the kitchen. I try to fight back, and I manage to get out the words, "Please stop, NO, you are hurting me!"

He forces his lips on mine to keep me from talking. His hand grabs my breast under my shirt as his hard penis comes between my legs. I push him away and he comes at me again. He mutters menacingly, "I will be fast, Lincee. I won't hurt you. Just relax. I want you now! I want you so badly!"

He pushes me down, holding my head down against the counter with a fist full of my long, silky black hair in his hand to keep me under his control. I think to myself, "When is this going to end?" I can't speak, my head is hurting, and I feel something drip down my leg as he lets out a huge gasp of ecstasy. He finally lets go of my hair and speaks vulgarity to me as I lay limp not moving. He says in a deep, low voice against my cheek, "Don't worry, Lincee. It's your word against mine. There are no cameras here." He swiftly picks up my ripped panties and tosses it in the large bin where the pizza dough is normally kept, then quickly walks out of the pizzeria galley. I do not recall how long I am alone. I eventually regain my strength and limp back to my cabin below deck. I am in such shock that I do not even know how I made it back to my cabin. It is over! I am safe for now.

Early next morning, the pizzeria chef makes a report to the Security Department that there was a break-in at the kitchen galley. As the investigation proceeds, the only thing the security personnel find is a pair of ripped panties in a pizza dough bin. There is no other evidence that points to the true story. Nothing was stolen or misplaced, so the investigation ceases with a warning to all department heads to lock each premise at the end of the day. This news spreads like wildfire through all the departments, and I hear it the morning when I arrive for my shift. I do not say one single word as I cannot even hold my head up feeling such heavy shame and disgrace.

That afternoon I walk to the Staff Mess for lunch with my team and, as we get off the elevator, the Croatian Officer is standing in front of me to get on. He sees me get off the crew elevator with my team and looks at me. He pulls at my arm to hold me back as the rest of my teammates walk ahead to the mess. I look at him and he mutters under his breath, "Did you hear about the security incident report from the pizzeria chef? They found your panties. You better not say anything." The smirk on his face makes me cringe as he walks away. My whole body freezes in shock for a moment as I look up at the ceiling and, to my dismay, see there are no cameras mounted by the elevator to record what has just happened. With a deep sigh, my shoulders sag as I head toward the Staff Mess for lunch, trying to hold in my tears.

As I walk down the corridor to catch up with my colleagues, I look up and see a bulletin board ahead of me. The poster in the centre of it catches my eye. "Christian fellowship tonight at 11:00 p.m. in the Staff Mess." I stop in front of the bulletin board to read the other notices for the crew and stare at the Christian fellowship flyer even though I see beside it another flyer for the Catholic Church service for crew offered that same Sunday night.

When at sea, to a crew member, the days all start to blend in together. Days become mentally marked "port day" or "sea day." I have lost track of the days of the week and even the week of the month. I suddenly realize I have been onboard only twelve days and today is Sunday. My heart leaps with just a little bit of excitement as I continue to read the details for the church service. I think to myself, "Perhaps I may find some peace and support at tonight's service for the crew. I may even make a friend." I long to meet a crew member with whom I can talk and pray with during this contract. At this point, I feel the need of prayer for my mind, soul, and body. As I sit down to eat my lunch, I realize I am scheduled again to work the late shift and I will have to miss tonight's church service. My heart sinks as my teeth sink into my cheeseburger. I make a mental note to attend the church service the following Sunday.

It has been a long fifteen-hour day sailing at sea and I am glad to be done with the passengers. I am ready for some peace and quiet in my cabin. My roommate, Katerina, is always out partying in the Crew Bar after work, and my department colleagues have their own social lives outside of work hours. Despite finding some solace hiding in the chapel and playing the piano, I long to find a friend with whom I can share my heart and journey with. At the end of each day, I try to find comfort in my cabin when the neighbor's music is not blaring or the stench of heavily-worn shoes does not waft into my cabin because every night all the crew members' shoes are propped up along the corridors for airing out. The trash and recycling bins frequently clang along the handrails in every corridor along the crew quarters, which also disturbs my peace. As I lay in bed listening to all the creaking noises of the ship and the splash of the waves against the cold wall beside my bunk, I shiver under my blanket and pray I will fall asleep before my roommate comes back drunk in the middle of the night.

Chapter 3

Contraband

Individually, we are one drop. Together we are on ocean.
Ryunosuke Satoro

After lunch, Katerina and I walk back to our cabins to rest before our next shift. Once we arrive in our tiny cabin on Deck Three, I go over to the sink to brush my teeth as Katerina flops on the bottom bunk bed. We are only three feet from each other as the sink is just outside the washroom door. In all the cabins on our deck, the sinks are outside of the washroom so one crew member can shower inside the washroom while the other bunkmate can brush their teeth and get ready for the day outside of the washroom.

Katerina asks, "Lincee, did you see the messages I left for you beside the phone last night?" As I stand in front of the sink brushing my teeth looking into the mirror inside our tiny cabin, I turn around with the toothbrush still in my hand as I continue to brush. I stop and reply, "What messages?" with toothpaste foaming between my lips. I put the toothbrush back in my mouth as Katerina reaches over to the desk beside our bunk bed and pulls up a piece of white paper. She lay on the bottom bunk as she reads the messages to me while I brush my teeth leaning on the bathroom door looking over at her.

"Lincee, I left you this paper by the telephone last night so that when you came home you could see all the calls you got." Katerina continues to read the messages as she turns over to lay on her stomach and I am bent over the sink rinsing out my toothpaste.

"Who are these people calling you? All these guys called yesterday for you!" Katerina continues, "Vladimir the Baker, Steven the Butcher, Sam the Electrician, John from the Room Service Department, Santiago from the Casino, Kenny from the Deck Department, and some guy named Alan. Lincee, who are all these men calling you?" Katerina asks in a somewhat surprised and bewildered tone of voice.

"What? Are you sure those calls are all for me, Katerina?" I reply as I put my toothbrush in the counter cup above the sink and then sit down on the chair beside her bed. I grab the piece of paper and look at all the names of the men she has scribbled down with their positions and their cabin numbers. My eyebrows raised, I continue, "Katerina, I don't know any of these people. I do not have friends on this ship. It has only been two weeks I have been onboard, and I have not made any friends. I know only you and the people I work with and Michael from the Bridge. I don't know how any of these crew members got my cabin number."

Katerina sits straight up, her head almost hitting my bunk above her. Her eyes open wide. "Lincee, what are you saying? All these men know our cabin number and are calling asking for you! I told them you weren't home last night, then some up of them came up to me in the Crew Bar asking for you. Who is Michael, this Bridge Officer you are talking about? How did you meet him? What's going on, Lincee?" Before I even try to answer all of Katerina's questions, she continues, "The other day when you placed your cheeseburger order in the Staff Mess, you freely gave our cabin number to some random crew member and look what happened! All the men now are calling our cabin for you. You must never give our cabin number to anyone unless they are your friend, okay? Do not make this mistake again, okay Lincee? Did you give our cabin number to anyone else?" She finally stops peppering me with questions.

I sheepishly look at Katerina and quietly apologize for my mistake. I tell Katerina that Officer Michael from the Bridge heard me playing the piano the other day in the chapel and came inside to talk with me. Katerina excitedly replies, "Lucky you! You met an officer from the Bridge! Can you get us a tour of the Bridge? Maybe we can meet the Captain." Crew members think that getting to meet an officer from the Bridge is like trying to meet a rock star—hard to reach and impossible to get a tour from. The Bridge is off limits to crew in other departments since the events of September 11, 2001. The world and security operate differently now, and everyone knows that getting to visit the Bridge is a privilege only given through invitation by the Captain or who you know through connections. I have no intentions of going to the Bridge. I certainly do not want to run into that Croatian

Bridge Officer. I am content meeting Officer Michael in the privacy of the chapel for our weekly piano lessons.

That night after our shift, Katerina and I lay in our bunk beds talking until midnight before finally drifting off to sleep. Suddenly, the telephone rings. Katerina, who is closest to the telephone on the desk, reaches over and answers it. "Hello?...Lincee, it's for you." Groggy in my sleep, I turn over and reach down from my bunk to take the phone from Katerina's hand. "Hello?...No, thank you. I am sleeping now. Bye." I reach down far to place the receiver back on the phone.

Twenty minutes later, the telephone rings again and wakes the both of us up. Katerina reaches over once more and picks up the receiver answering in a sleepy voice, "Hello?... Lincee, it's for you."

I turn over and reach down again to grab the phone. "Hello?...No, thank you. I am sleeping now. Bye." I hang up.

Thirty minutes later, the telephone rings and rings. Katerina is in a deep sleep and snoring and refuses to be woken up to answer it. I try to ignore the ringing, hoping it will stop, but it doesn't. Katerina finally stops snoring and reaches over the phone. This time she does not even say "Hello." She calls out my name, "Lincee, it's for you."

I pick up the phone receiver and hang up without even saying a word, then pull the plug out of the jack on the wall.

The next morning the alarm beeps at 7:00 a.m. and both of us are not finished sleeping. The damn telephone robbed us of our sleep and the constant ringing has made us both irritated as we start the day. As I start to climb down the ladder from my top bunk, Katerina says, "Lincee, who are all these men calling you in the middle of the night? They are disturbing our sleep! Tell them to stop calling at such a bad time. We are sleeping!"

I feel bad that all these calls are for me and I don't even know the crew members who are calling. I calmly reply to Katerina, "I really don't know who these men are, Katerina. They called last night to invite me to the Crew Bar for a drink and some dancing."

Katerina started her contract a few weeks prior to my joining the ship. She had the cabin to herself and so, since I joined approximately two weeks ago, I feel like I am in her territory. She is like a big sister to me. She knows the ropes, the ranks, and the fellow crew members much better than me. She spends time in the Crew Bar every night socializing, so she knows many people from all departments. I am still learning how to survive at sea. I don't know many things; I don't even know how to report a noise complaint or any other issue or concern. Whenever we finish our shift, Katerina goes about her social life, which often leaves me alone to make my own friends. Most times I go to the chapel to practice the piano or walk some laps around deck. That is pretty much the extent of my life outside of work.

Tonight, I am excited to attend the Christian fellowship Bible study in hopes of making some new friends. It is Wednesday, and the flyer on the bulletin board invited crew members for Christian Bible study on Wednesdays and weekly church service on Sundays. I missed out on last Sunday's service due to working the late shift, so today is the first chance I have to possibly make some friends outside of my department.

After work, Katerina and I go directly to our cabin and she tells me to order room service and to ask for John. "Lincee, John knows you! He called you the other day and if you call him back, he can get us some passenger food. Room service for us crew! Call him." Katerina is changing out of her uniform into her dancing clothes. We are both hungry and there is no food in the mess for us at 10:30 p.m. Only alcohol is served to crew in the Crew Bar, and I feel I owe Katerina this one favour.

"I don't want to call this guy John. He is working the room service for passengers! That food is for passengers, not crew. I cannot call and ask for delivery for us; we are crew. I will get in trouble," I reply as I lay stretched out on my bunk still in my uniform.

"Are you hungry, Lincee? Please call and order a hot sandwich for us and some potato chips. I will pay!" Katerina pleads with me.

"If I call and ask for this favour, this guy John is going to want something in return for this request." I already know what this sailor will want in return and I refuse to give him even the slightest idea that sex is an option. I certainly do not want to be in any debt to some random crew member named John in the Food and Beverage Department. If anyone wants anything on this ship, it's all about trading amongst the sailors. A deep, secret, underground black market exists amongst all sailors of every rank in every department, all unbeknownst to passengers and the Head Office. Sexual favours are often expected in return for any type of contraband. I have seen crew members desperate for a phone card when the phone card machine is empty. I once heard that one crew member bought twenty phone cards and sold them for sexual favours. What would this John want of me for ordering contraband food meant for passengers?

After much urging on Katerina's part, I reluctantly pick up the telephone and order two hot sandwiches for us. Within five minutes, there is a knock at our cabin door. John from passenger room service sent the delivery guy to our cabin with a plate of two hot sandwiches and potato chips wrapped in plastic wrap, all hidden in a giant, paper laundry bag meant for passenger use. Delivering food of any type anywhere for crew is considered contraband and is always delivered in a large, white, paper laundry bag to disguise it as laundry delivery. When navigating through the ship with a laundry bag, no passenger or officer suspects anything amiss. People just think you are carrying laundry. Today I learn the laundry bag fits a large plate of delicious, hot food for our cabin. Taking passenger food to crew quarters is considered contraband and can result in a severe warning or even dismissal if caught. I stand behind the door as Katerina opens it. She reached for the laundry bag as she hands over $4 USD. Two dollars for each order. The crew member asks Katerina, "Where's Lincee? The order is for her," as he holds the laundry bag horizontal to ensure the plate of sandwiches stays intact.

Katerina replies, "Thanks, I will give it to her. Bye!" She shuts the cabin door with the bag in hand. I can feel the warmth of the plate with the hot food on top as I remove the large paper bag. The aroma of passenger sandwiches with a side of potato chips wafts throughout our tiny cabin. We both giggle as we scarf down the warm meal to fill our hungry stomachs. I feel like we have just committed a crime, that we did something illegal. We paid money to our fellow crew member who pocketed it for himself for providing goods that were meant for passengers. This is a win-win situation for all crew involved. Now I am part of the underground black market, a part of the underground food mafia. Katerina prepares to go off to the Crew Bar to disco while I think of a way to transport this plate back to passenger quarters without being caught.

It's almost 11:00 p.m. when Katerina and heads out for some dancing and cheap alcohol. "Lincee, you coming to the Crew Bar tonight?"

"No, thanks for the invite. I don't like all the cigarette smoke and loud music. See you tomorrow, have fun!" I smile back as Katerina leaves the cabin.

As soon as she is gone, I climb up the ladder to my top bunk, grab my Bible from under my pillow, and put it inside my bag with my large bottle of water. I also put the plate back inside the white laundry bag to toss in the pantry on my way to the Staff Mess at the back of the ship. With a full stomach, I feel so happy and excited to head out to the mess to meet some fellow crew members for Bible study and possibly make a friend. I do not even bother to change out of my uniform. I quickly walk down the i95 corridor that stretches the entire length of the ship along Deck Four. When I arrive in Zone Five at the back of the ship, I pull open the glass doors to the Staff Mess. First, I pop my head inside and then I stumble into the room feeling a bit nervous to see about twenty men. Some are still in uniform and some in their civvies since they had time to change after their shift. I ask, "Is this the Christian Bible study tonight?"

I am warmly invited to join the fellow crew members. I am greeted as "Sister Lincee" as each person comes up to me with outstretched hands to meet me. They already all know my name even though my long, black hair covers the name badge placed above my left breast. I am surprised by such a warm greeting and a sense of peace overcomes my heart. I finally feel at home. I notice not one single woman is present, but I still feel safe. I suddenly remember to look up at the ceiling surreptitiously searching for cameras only to remember there are no cameras in the crew areas and most definitely not in the Staff Mess.

For the next hour and a half, I am at ease because we speak the language of God's love. I finally feel like I've made some friends this evening. Brother Matthew from the Philippines asks me to close the evening in prayer. They are all pleased that I had the courage to join and come out to the Bible study rather than go lounging and dancing in the Crew Bar. My choice of pastime is certainly not to be in a loud, music-blaring, smoke-filled environment with drunken sailors lusting over the few women onboard in the tight quarters of the Crew Bar located in the bellows of the ship on Deck Two. After a long day of entertaining passengers, I thirst for a quiet environment and I long for spiritual and intellectual nourishment. I believe I have finally found a place onboard at sea to help me get through this contract.

After Bible study, Brother Matthew kindly walks me back to my cabin as we exchange pleasantries about our Christian upbringing. Once alone inside, I climb up to my top bunk, finally feeling a sense of peace. Although it is only Wednesday, I am already excited for Sunday to arrive for the next Christian fellowship. It is such a good way to end the day; my stomach is full, my mind has been intellectually stimulated, and my heart and soul are fed with the Word of God. I quickly fall into a deep sleep as the Alaskan waters splash up against the other side of my cabin wall and the ship gently sways me to sleep like a baby with each swell.

Bang! Bang! Bang! I hear three heavy fists hit my cabin door which startles me out of a deep sleep. I turn over and hide my head under my blankets. Bang! Bang! Bang! Again, on my cabin door sounds the loud knocking. I ignore it and hope it will stop. Then I hear Katerina's voice in a slurred yet very loud voice, "Lincee, open up the door! I lost my key!"

I climb down the ladder to open the door for her. Katerina stumbles in completely drunk. She does not even look at me or say anything. She just flops face down onto her bunk and passes out in her dancing clothes. I close the cabin door and lock it. Without a word, I climb back up the ladder to my bed. I cannot seem to fall back asleep as I am not pleased that she startled me out of a deep sleep and now is snoring very loudly. "God, help me!" I start to pray as I lay in my bed.

Chapter 4
Missing Laundry

Life's roughest storms prove the strength of our anchor. Anonymous

Doing laundry on land was a relaxing weekly chore I welcomed after a long week. Saturday mornings, I would carefully and calmly sort my laundry into piles while separating the dark colours and whites—a mundane yet quiet and calm routine. Frankly, I enjoyed this simple task that most people I know loathe. I always had enough liquid laundry soap, enough space to sort my laundry, and I could do as many loads of laundry I wanted without a care that the laundry machine would leak or break down or that any items would go missing. I never worried that someone else would come along and touch or steal my laundry. Little did I know that I would one day wish doing laundry was as relaxing and simple as it had always been until it was the day I had to do laundry at sea.

On this cruise ship, I learn there are only four washers and dryers for the officers located in the officer quarters on Deck Ten. There are four washers and dryers for the rank of the staff crew members located in the middle of the ship on Deck Four. Below deck, meaning under the water line, there are only four washers and dryers for the rest of the crew members on Deck Two at the bow of the ship. On this ship, we have 1,200 passengers with their own laundry facilities that are strictly reserved for passenger use. There are 670 crew members and only three laundry stations for three ranks to do our own laundry. Uniforms can be sent to the main laundry to be cleaned for free, but you have to wait for them to be washed and ready for pick up or returned to you which is generally within three days, two days if you are lucky and have connections.

I quickly realize I can send my uniform out to be washed and still have two sets of uniforms to get me through till the next cycle if I do not have any accidents that dirty my clothes. But then there is the issue of washing my undergarments, my civilian clothes, pillowcase, and personal towel. This will be a challenge with only access to four washing machines and competing with all the crew members. I certainly do not have the luxury of separating my laundry into the three separate piles for three machines when I want to clean my clothes. So this afternoon, I commence the adventure of doing laundry at sea. I walk to the midship deck to the laundry room reserved for the staff crew members with laundry bag in tow and a small box of laundry soap I purchased in the crew sundries shop.

I personally do not like powder laundry soap, but that is all that is sold in the sundry shop for the crew. Packing laundry soap in one's luggage and towing it from home to the ship is not an option even considered. Every inch of space in one's luggage is carefully and precisely filled with only the bare necessities. Purchasing laundry soap on the ship is the best option for crew members. Most crew members only pack one piece of luggage and one carry-on for an entire contract, which can last up to ten months at sea. With a tiny cabin to share and limited space, crew members must learn to boil to it down to an exact science of only packing the bare necessities to get through their time on ship. Toiletries and laundry soap can always be bought in the sundry shop or on land, though there is no guarantee that there will be any supplies in stock or you'll get the brand of your choice.

I walk into the laundry room on Deck Four at midship only to see that all four machines are in use and there is a lineup of about ten crew members ahead of me. The laundry room is no larger than twenty by fifteen feet. The machines are stacked and there is a small table for ironing. To my dismay, I can already see I will not get my laundry done here within my three-hour break. I walk out of the laundry room and think to try the laundry room for the rank below me in the crew quarters in Zone One below deck. I navigate myself through the labyrinth maze along Deck Two to the very front of the ship and finally locate the laundry room. It seems like it took me twenty minutes just to locate it. I pass many crew members on Deck Two as I ask for directions to the laundry room. Little do I know that all these crew members watching me walk along the corridors with my big bag of laundry in tow have a single, menacing thought in mind. I am the rat that willingly walked into this maze below deck and the hungry cats are ready and eager to pounce on this unsuspecting crew member.

I finally arrive at the heavy steel door in Zone One that has the small label on the top right corner of the door indicating I've reached the laundry. I push against the heavy door while trying to balance my laundry bag and soap, then stumble inside the small room. I see all four machines are in use and two people are ahead of me. I am relieved that I can hopefully get my laundry done within my three-hour break which has now dwindled down to two and a half hours. As I stand in the tight-knit quarters, I watch one crew member take clothes out of the washer when the machine is complete and dump the wet clothes on the ironing table. Then he puts his dirty laundry inside the washer machine, slams the door, pushes some buttons, and walks out of the room. Then, another crew member takes out the clothes in the dryer that has just stopped and tosses them on the ironing board next to the pile of wet clothes. He next puts his own wet clothes in the dryer, then leaves the laundry room. I certainly do not like what I have just witnessed. These crew members did not even wait for the owner of the clothes to remove their own belongings out of the machine; they just removed the clean clothes themselves and dumped it on the dirty ironing board which I can see is filthy with countless stains of various colours.

There is not one single minute to waste at sea. If you are not present to remove your own clothes from the machine the moment it stops, someone else will remove it for you and who knows where that crew member may dump them or even where their hands have been. One machine becomes available and it is finally my turn. I certainly do not have the luxury to sort and use three machines as time is of the essence and now there are two crew members in line behind me waiting. With only one washing machine available for all my dirty clothes, I decide to load everything into it and pray that the colours do not run into my whites. I look at the watch on my wrist and make a mental note to come back before the thirty-minute mark when the machine stops. I certainly do not want another person's hands touching my private, delicate attire.

I turn to head back to my cabin to pick up the fabric static sheet; I had packed a few Bounce sheets in my luggage. As I leave Zone One at the front of the ship, I head toward my cabin in Zone Three in the middle of the ship. I decide to pay closer attention to the cabin numbers and the number of left and right turns I must take along Deck Two. Once again, I feel like I am in a rat maze, but this time it is the afternoon and many crew members are on break with their cabin doors propped open. From one, I can hear the television blaring as I walk by; I hear music from another. There are people chatting in various languages in the hallways as I continue to walk by. With each step I take, I can smell the stench of shoes propped along the corridors and hear the trash bins banging along the handrail as the ship ever so slightly sways back and forth with each swell of the ocean water. The assault on my senses makes me crave some fresh air and sunlight. All the crew members I walk by stare at me with their lusting eyes, drooling at me like a piece of meat as I quickly walk through each zone below deck in my uniform.

Crew members of another rank generally do not walk in the same space as the rank below them, so for me to be in the midst of the crew on Deck Two draws some unwelcome attention. This is especially because I am in their territory, using their laundry facilities. I uncomfortably feel like a prostitute walking along a dark alley of hungry, sex-starved sailors. I do not see one single female crew member until I come up above onto Deck Four. I shudder and am relieved to be above the water line now walking along the i95 where there is more traffic here and with other fellow crew members in my own rank. A female nurse walks by me as I pass the Medical Centre, and I go down the flight of stairs to my own cabin.

On this ship, I learn that the ratio of male to female crew members is astoundingly uneven, though this is as expected on all the ships across the fleet. The few female crew members who work on this ship are comprised of eight in the dining room, six buffet stewards, two in the boutique shops, four in the spa, four dancers, one singer, a few cabin stewards, the few of us in the Entertainment Department, two in the Security Department, and the two nurses in the Medical Centre. There are 670 crew onboard and approximately forty females now since turnaround day. Men are always the dominant sex at sea. The common image of the sailor is a man who is tough enough to handle the rough seas, the long workdays that turn into months, and the repetitive, labour-intensive, demanding work. Most women still consider working on land the preferential choice. In the past, very few women sought employment at sea, but slowly over the years, the landscape and lucrative offers in the cruise industry have enticed more women to consider a life at sea as a better option than working in their own home country. Many of the female crew members hope to find a rich sailor from another foreign land to marry.

I am just the opposite, and I certainly do not have any agenda at sea other than looking for an adventure and something different to break up my mundane routine back home. I have no desire or even the thought to seek another life in another country through the means of shacking up with a sex-starved sailor. I am here because I had grown tired of training clients at the gym who did not take the fitness program plan I set for them seriously, so starting a new chapter at sea is what I thought would break the monotony and spice up my life just a little bit. I know after this short-term contract; I will go back home again to fill the time.

My time has been enjoyable working in the Entertainment Department. Most importantly, I am enjoying sailing because all my meals are prepared for me. I don't have to plan what I am going to eat, go grocery shopping, cook, or even do dishes. I feel pampered at sea as everything is done for me whereas back home on land I have to do everything for myself because I live alone. My cabin steward comes daily into my cabin to make my bed, clean my living quarters, and bring fresh towels. Growing up, I was raised to always make my bed, so cleaning up after myself has been ingrained in me since I was a child. Therefore, I ask my cabin steward to never touch my bed as I certainly do not want anyone's hands fluffing my blankets and touching my pillowcase after cleaning the toilet. The housekeeping steward is still eager to earn a few extras dollars despite my request to lighten his workload in my cabin. I assure him that my weekly gratuity for him will not decrease and all my requests are kindly met with courtesy and respect just as he serves the passengers in kind.

After watching about twenty minutes of television, I jump down from my bunk and grab the fabric static sheet from inside my closet that I had carefully packed inside a Ziploc sandwich bag. I navigate my way toward Zone One back to the laundry room. As I pass by the many male crew members below deck, I am stopped by a few of them trying to chat me up. Every few steps I take, I am stopped by another crew member asking me questions. I smile politely and quickly answer the questions, but I am delayed getting to the laundry room in time to take my clothes out of the machine. When I finally arrive, I am dismayed to see my wet clothes on the dirty ironing board and two crew members standing around pacing, waiting for an available machine. Whoever took my clothes out of the washer has already left. I am not pleased as I stand waiting for a dryer. Finally, one becomes available and I put my wet clothes in it with the static sheet. I look at my watch, then head towards the crew elevator to avoid having to walk back along Deck Two and run into those male crew members again.

I take the elevator up to the eighth floor and walk out down the corridor toward the outdoor deck sectioned off for crew. I walk through the Crew Bar and, as I pass by the bar station, I notice the hours of operation sign posted on the wall by the bar. The bar opens at 11:00 p.m. every night. I make a mental note to come back at the end of the day to purchase a few bottles of water. The stench of stale cigarette smoke still reeks from last night's crew disco and the floor is still sticky from the spilled alcohol. I see two used condoms in the corner by the couches as I walk past heading toward the heavy steel door to get to the outside deck. I am so relieved to finally get some fresh air, enjoy a few moments of solitude, and feel the sunshine on my face as I breathe in deeply the Alaskan salty sea air. I lick my dry lips and taste the salt of the ocean on them. I realize I am thirsty and start to head back to my cabin for some water. I remind myself again that I am running low on water bottles and to not forget to buy bottled water tonight after my shift when the Crew Bar first opens.

As I leave the crew deck, I must walk through the bar again across the sticky floor in order to get back to the crew elevator. As I turn the corner, suddenly the Croatian Officer steps out in front of me. I stop and freeze.

"Well hello, Lincee! How are you doing?"

I am in such shock that I am speechless, not knowing what to say. No words come out of my mouth. I look around and see no other crew members; I look up and see no cameras on the ceiling.

He continues in his thick Croatian accent, "Where are you going, Lincee? What are you doing here on Deck Eight?"

I try to walk past him, but he blocks my way and waits till I answer his questions. I manage to stammer out, "I came to buy some water, but the Crew Bar is not open. Excuse me, I have to go pick up my laundry." I step to the other side of him and try to pass but he blocks me again.

"I can give you a bottle of water, Lincee" he answers back in his thick accent.

"No thanks. I will buy it from the Crew Bar tonight," I reply with disgust.

"Come with me, Lincee. I can show you where to get a bottle of water right now for free." He smiles more widely at me as his words drip with the intensity of a sailor starved for sex. Then, he suddenly grabs my hand and pulls me hard behind the heavy steel door. I panic as I try to pull my hand away. He calmly says to me as he yanks me down the quiet officer's corridor, "Lincee, I will not hurt you. I will give you a bottle of water. Just come with me."

I know what he wants in exchange for a bottle of water. I am not that desperate even though my throat and lips are dry, and I can still taste the salt of the ocean lingering on my lips. All I can think of is how to get out of this situation and back to my laundry downstairs.

He pushes me towards a white door which turns out to be his cabin. I cannot find a way out of this precarious situation as he blocks me at every turn when I try to break free. He then pulls my arm inside his cabin and tries to relax me with his words.

"Lincee, look, I have a bottle of water for you," he says as he reaches down by his large queen-sized bed. "I am going home this turnaround day as my contract ends and I won't be able to drink all this water. You can have it," he continues as he sits on his bed, looking longingly at me.

I stand in silence by the door ready to make a break as our eyes lock. He slowly stands up from his bed and walks towards me as my hand slowly reaches for the door handle to flee. "Don't fight me, Lincee. I want you one last time before I disembark. I won't hurt you. I just want your body and to feel you again." He immediately puts the weight of his hand on the door so I cannot pull it open, leaning his body into mine.

I turn my head as he tries to kiss me, but my back is against the door and I am trapped. I feel his other hand tear open my uniform shorts as his other hand slides down my shoulder to squeeze a fistful of my left breast.

I am stuck! I try to push back, but his hands are very strong. I can feel his hard body up against me as I grab his hands to push him away. He pulls me hard towards the bed and throws me down; it happens so fast. I try to turn over and get up, but he is already on top of me.

"Lincee! Oh, Lincee. I want you so bad! I want to feel you! Don't fight me!" he menacingly whispers into my neck as his hands pin me down on his bed and he has his way with me.

A sailor at sea is often pent up with a large, hungering need for sex, and this Croatian Officer has a lusting interest in my body. His sweat is all over me. I feel so gross and disgusted. His body weight is pressing heavy against my chest. I do not have a voice to utter any sounds or even the ability to cry as I fight back. I am in such shock about the violent assault unfolding. I feel so used and dirty.

After what seems like forever, I manage to get back to Deck Two only to find my dry pile of laundry on the dirty ironing board. It has been forty-five minutes, and someone took my laundry out of the dryer without a care. Without a word, I grab my laundry with both arms and go back to my cabin with my head down. I toss the clean laundry on my top bunk and jump into the shower to wash away his scent, sweat, and sperm off me. I am still in shock as to what has just transpired that I start crying in the shower while washing feverishly with soap. I stand in the shower stall under the hot water for quite some time trying to make myself feel clean. After I dry myself off, I wrap my towel around me so I can air out between my legs. As I start to fold my laundry, I notice some missing items and, to my utter dismay, I only find one pair of underwear in the pile.

At this point, I am utterly distraught as I am most certain I had put two weeks' worth of underwear in the laundry. I frantically search for my missing underwear in the pile of clean clothes. Someone had stolen my underwear! I now only have this one pair of clean underwear and the ripped one I was left to wear when I escaped the Croatian Officer's cabin. I am beyond upset and shocked as tears stream down my face anew. My hands are shaking as I carefully folded my laundry. My breast is sore from his hard squeeze and I can still smell the scent of him on me even though I washed thoroughly with soap. Where in the world am I going to get clean underwear? This is now my next problem besides getting more bottled water. I can always buy bottled water from the Crew Bar at the end of the day if there is any left after my shift, but where in the world can I buy underwear? Every port of call where we dock on this ship's itinerary is littered with tourist souvenir shops. Where does one buy underwear? Most certainly one cannot borrow underwear or even a toothbrush from another crew member! Now I must wash my underwear by hand every night until I can figure out where to purchase new ones.

Chapter 5

Ministry Unveiled

They that go down to the ship, that do business in great waters; these see the works of the Lord, and His wonders in the deep. Psalm 107:23-24

As the ship pulls into the port of Juneau, my roommate tells me there is a shuttle for the crew that charges $10 USD for a round-trip to Walmart. She is going to pick up some toiletries and asks if I want to come along. I have never felt so excited to go shopping for underwear and some much-needed comfort food. Chocolate and potato chips are my go-to foods and just what I crave to soothe my sorrow away. They are on my shopping list right next to underwear. I have stopped going to the gym to work out because, since I joined the ship, I do not care anymore about my exercise routine or eating healthy or even being a role model to my clients at the gym. Junk food, pizza, and burgers are what I crave at sea. On land, I never touch such foods. But here at sea, the pizza grill and the burger joint are just too enticing that I cannot resist the food freshly made for me. At sea, I find that there is not enough time to exercise or to be selective of what to eat. With the spare time I do have, I want to practice the piano in the chapel and attend Bible studies on Wednesday nights and church service on Sundays. I am craving fellowship with people of the same mind and heart.

When the shuttle van arrives at the doorstep of Walmart, all of us crew members jump out and go our separate ways to purchase what we want. The shuttle will be back at the same drop off location in one hour, so time is of the essence. As I walk up and down the aisles, I cannot believe the low prices of shampoo, laundry soap, chocolate, and clothes. The prices are much lower than the Walmart back home. My priority is to stock up on at least two weeks' worth of underwear in case I do not have time to do laundry. I stock up on toiletries and decide to purchase some new clothes to make myself feel better as I really do not know when I will have time to come out to Walmart again. After the shuttle drops us off at the pier by the ship, I walk up the hill to the payphone and make my collect calls home to my sister and mom. Then it is a quick trip to the Juneau public library to use the computers to check email. Being ashore for a crew member is always a time crunch with errands to run plus the search for Wi-Fi and a quiet place to call home.

As I head back to the ship, I pray God will help heal my mind, body, and soul. I desperately want to prove to myself that I have the resilience and fortitude to overcome any obstacle thrown at me and that I can survive a life at sea. If I could survive my ordeals back home on land over the past thirty years, I most certainly want to believe wholeheartedly that I can finish this contract with my head held high. I feel a sense of determination take hold in my mind and heart to confront and speak up if I am ever attacked again.

I am relieved the Croatian Officer is going home this Sunday, as it is turnaround day. Every turnaround day, our ship brings on new passengers. Crew members who have finished their contracts will go home as a new set of crew members join to replace them. This is the norm every turnaround day as new joiners replace the leavers. The Croatian Officer's contract is coming to an end, and I feel great relief to know I will not have to face him again for the remainder of my contract. His presence alone made for a silent, insidious threat. I did not dare tell Michael, the other Bridge Officer, about his Croatian colleague. Michael and I enjoy our weekly piano lessons in the chapel whenever we can arrange a mutual time to meet when the chapel is free. Unfortunately, Michael is going home in two weeks as his contract is coming to an end. I am going to lose my only friend on this ship.

I still have a few hours before my next shift, and all the passengers and crew are still ashore. I grab my music folder and head towards the chapel. As I approach, I can hear someone playing the piano inside. I peer through the glass slats and catch the view through the other set of glass windows on the other end of the chapel. Our ship is still docked in

Juneau and I can see the mountain peaks through the triple-paned glass on that wall. My eyes gaze at the piano and I see a gentleman sitting on the piano bench. I first knock and then open the heavy chapel door to respectfully step inside.

I am relieved to see it is a crew member and not a passenger. We exchange introductions and pleasantries. I learn his name is Terrance and he is one of the resident pianists on the ship. We discuss the schedule of the chapel so we each can have turns to practice while the passengers are ashore. A sense of peace and joy overcomes my heart as I think to myself that I finally have made a friend who is a fellow musician of the same caliber and mindset as myself. I will finally be able to have some stimulating and intelligent conversations that my mind longs to have. Michael is going home soon, and now I've made a newfound friend named Terrance whom I hope will be a nice person.

It is Sunday evening and my shift finishes at 10:00 p.m., so I stop by the buffet designated for the passengers and enjoy my deck privileges of being able to eat this food despite it being not very fresh from sitting in heated pans since 5:30 p.m. Nonetheless, I enjoy this food instead of the old, stale food in the Crew Mess. I have nothing to complain about as I know I have it much better than most of the crew members in the rank below me. After eating, I rush back to my cabin to freshen up and head to tonight's Christian fellowship with my water bottle and Bible in tow. I am filled with excitement to have the opportunity to fellowship with crew members who have the same heart as myself.

The church service for the crew is again held in the Staff Mess, and my heart is leaping with excitement and joy as I open the heavy door. I step inside and am greeted by fellow crew who also have finished their shifts for the day. Many are out of their uniforms so no name badge sits on their left breast; I must try to remember each of their names as we greet one another. I did not have time to change out of uniform, and even though my long, silky, black hair is covering my name badge, everyone seems to know my name as we shake hands.

The ambience is totally different during these evening services than it normally is when I come into the Staff Mess for meals during the day. A pulpit is set up between the tables and speakers are set up for the musicians, who I now see are warming up their guitars. I see one of the dining tables on the side of the room is topped up with Bibles and the offering plate. Beside the pile of Bibles, I see the communion bread and wine. I hold my back my tears as I take a seat, my heart filling with a sense of peace and belonging. Tonight, I am longing to take communion, praying that the bread of Christ heals my body and the cup of Christ washes away my sins and my feelings of disgust from that officer. I want to be washed white as snow and become pure again. Upon sitting, I dare to ask another fellow crew member, "Where are the women? Are there any sisters-in-Christ onboard?"

Matthew, who is from the Philippines, assures me that there are two other women who attend fellowship, but sometimes they do not come as they are extremely tired after a fifteen-hour day shift and tonight they are not feeling well. I long to meet another woman of God on this ship even though I have met a few male Christians to fellowship with twice a week. As a few more crew members trickle in the Staff Mess, Matthew approaches me and asks me to open in prayer for this evening's service. I am shocked because I did not get advance notice and service is about to commence in five minutes. My heart is eager, and my mind is ready, but my lips and throat suddenly feel parched with nervousness. I can still taste the Alaskan ocean salt on my lips from when I walked along the deck earlier this evening. I grab my water bottle out of my bag and take a large gulp before I approach the podium to lead in prayer. I make a mental note to purchase more water as I am running low. Bottled water and crew calling phone cards are a commodity at sea, and I must make sure I make the time to pick up both while there are plenty in stock. Right now, I am about to open in prayer for the service, so I lick my lips one last time.

I approach the pulpit and a hush of silence overcomes the room. I speak clearly and in my teacher voice I greet everyone, "Good evening, my name is Lincee. Please join me in prayer." I bow my head and start the evening's service. At the conclusion of the service, I feel a huge sense of peace wash over me, from the crown of my head to the soles of my feet. Brother Matthews's sermon was such food for my soul and mind. I have longed to fellowship with other believers, and I realize that this part of my time onboard will be the much-needed encouragement I've yearned for to get through the remaining time of my contract. As the service ends, we say our final words. The crew trickle out and Brother Matthew approaches me to talk.

"Lincee, I am going home next turnaround day and we need another person to take over some responsibilities. Would you deliver the sermons and lead the Bible studies for the crew?" Matthew looks intently into my eyes as he speaks.

The first thoughts that come to my mind are that I am not qualified. I am not theologically trained in seminary school. A slight pause hangs in the air after he questions me and I manage to stammer out the words, "Brother Matthew, I am not qualified."

He replies, "Your English is perfect, your heart is right with God, and your mind is sharp. You are a teacher by training back home and know how to teach clients at the gym. God will provide the words for you. Pray about it and let me know as soon as possible. We need a strong leader to take over and assist in the fellowship for the crew. I am going home next turnaround day." Matthew reassures me that I can do it as he walks me back to my cabin and we further discuss the responsibilities of the Christian fellowship leaders.

As I lay in my top bunk shivering under the blankets thinking about this evening's service, I realize I forgot to buy a phone card and bottles of water from the Crew Bar to get me through the day tomorrow. The ship is swaying with the swells of the Alaskan waters and the steel hull of the ship is constantly grinding and making creaking noises. I feel like I am going to roll right out of the top bunk if it wasn't for the high railing against the edge of my bed. I feel so cold, and the creaking noises are robbing of me the much-needed rest my body craves. Such assaults on the senses have already deprive this sailor of solid sleep. Looking at my desk clock, I see it is past 1:00 a.m. and I desperately just want to sleep. My mind is wandering, so I start to pray for wisdom. I know in my heart I am called to serve God wherever my feet take me and today, at thirty years old, my feet have taken me here on this Alaskan cruise ship. As I reflect upon the many years of my decisions and plans, it has always been the Lord who has faithfully directed my steps in every aspect of my education, relationships, family, job opportunities, and whatever life's trials have thrown at me. Many times, I am surprised and blessed beyond measure, and I am thankful that the Lord kept certain doors closed for my own benefit even though I did not understand at the time. Looking back over the years I have walked with the Lord; I now see clearly how He has carefully planned and directed my journey.

So here I am on a luxury cruise ship, laying on a top bunk that sways with every swell of the waters coupled with the constant creaking noises of the ship. I never thought in a million years that I would be asked to deliver sermons to the people of God. These are big shoes to fill, and my mind wanders back to all the years I attended church growing up, watching, and listening to all those pastors deliver their sermons from the pulpit.

I grew up attending a Baptist church. After my father disappeared, my mother sought emotional, spiritual, and mental support from the church. In the eyes of my mother's family, for us kids to grow up in a single-parent family was a fall from grace, despite us being surrounded by all the broken families in my community. In my family, we were expected to always keep face and put forth an image that all was well and perfect. My mother could not sweep this family secret under the carpet, so she brought us to church for the support she needed. My first introduction to God was at the tender age of six and it was the first step in my spiritual journey seeking meaning in life. Every Sunday, Mom would take my siblings and me to church where she attended service upstairs in the sanctuary with the adults whereas my siblings and I attended Sunday school downstairs.

This was the first time I was told about God. I was told I am loved and cherished by Him. These were words I had never heard from an adult. We knew Mom loved us because she showed it in her determined actions of raising all of us while working two jobs and through her many sacrifices as a single parent. I watched my mother cry many times, calling out to God for help to put food on the table or praying that she would have enough money to pay the bills until the next payday. Over the years, I saw God deliver and meet each need for our family. Every night, Mom would gather my siblings and me and we would kneel along the bedside. She would pray, and each of us would take turns praying as well. All those years of watching my mother struggle and toil to raise us is a testimony of faith in and of itself.

Even though Dad disappeared into thin air and the police could not find his body, Mom raised us alone without any government assistance. Mom was too proud to take handouts, and she demonstrated a work ethic and determination to raise us herself alone by keeping two jobs. Every day, I saw Mom pray and exercise her faith, and I have seen with my own eyes how God answered each and every prayer as the years passed. Yet, at the young age of six-years-old, and every day after kneeling by the bedside with my siblings, the only prayer that I wanted answered was for God to bring Daddy back to us and that Mom would not have to work so hard. As a kid growing up, I felt the absence of a parent every day; I dearly missed and needed my Daddy.

After a few years, my mother brought us to another church in the city. It was an Alliance church and where I got most of my upbringing in Sunday school during my elementary formative years. It was also where I was baptized. When I became a teenager, Mom brought us to a Pentecostal church for a few years. It wasn't until I reached university that I decided to attend the closest church to the campus, which was a Presbyterian church. Being a music student in the Faculty of Music, I yearned to play the piano as much as possible around the city. I was often called to fill in as the emergency pianist in different denominational churches in the area.

This opportunity let me see how the various denominations delivered the order of services and to hear different styles of sermons. I collected all sorts of genres of music for my repertoire, including all sorts of Christian hymns and praise songs. Playing the piano over the years in church gave me a sense of peace as I listened to the congregation sing. I always focused on hitting the right keys on the piano so much that I often did not sing the words to the piece.

I got to see how some Christian denominations delivered their communion services with one Chalice cup for the Blood of Christ and how the congregants would leave their pews and line up to the front of the church to each drink from the same cup. I call this the drive-thru method. I witnessed in other church denominations how the congregation stayed seated in their pews during communion while I played the hymns. The side persons or ushers would pass the communion tray with little cups filled with wine for each person to take out and eat with the given bread at the same time the pastor spoke. This was my cue to stop playing the piano. I call this the take-out method. When everyone drank together from their little cups and placed them in a pew cup holder, it was the cue that I could start playing the piano again.

All the little cues during each service were a guiding timeline for me as a pianist, and I learned quite a bit just by observing and visiting the different denominations within the Christian churches across the city. Attending various denominational and non-denominational churches while growing up taught me that it did not matter how the order of the service was conducted. All that mattered was that the Word of God was spoken, and that the Bible's message of salvation was delivered. The logistics of how communion was delivered, either drive-thru or take-out method, did not really matter.

"Train up a child in the way he should go, and when he is old he will not turn from it" (Proverbs 22:6 NIV).

Now that Brother Matthew has asked me to take over some of the leadership responsibilities, my heart is moved to follow where the Holy Spirit prompts me to move. I know I couldn't grieve the prompting of the Holy Spirit tugging at my heart with disobedience, and I truly want to remain obedient. I resolve that I am ready to move forward into this new chapter in my life, which now includes a life of ministry despite feeling ill-equipped to fill the role as a minister. I make a mental note to myself that I will make an appointment with the church rector and any pastor willing to speak with me when I return to back on land upon completing this contract. I will need some guidance if I am to continue with this torch handed over to me.

For now, I am at sea alone with no guidance on how to write a sermon and with much responsibility handed over to me on top of my regular duties as an entertainer for the passengers. I drift off to sleep as I pray for wisdom and direction. The next morning, I wake up knowing in my heart that

I will take over this role of ministry, which is purely voluntary outside of my work schedule and not a paid position or one even recognized by Head Office. I have only a few days to quickly learn the ropes on how to tread this role carefully as the wisdom of Brother Matthew is going home on Sunday.

"For Wisdom is more precious than rubies, and nothing you desire can compare with her" (Proverbs 8:11 NIV).

In the days that lead up to turnaround day, I spend as much time as I can with Brother Matthew, seeking his wisdom and advice. I prepare my first sermon in my spare time away from practicing the piano and entertaining the passengers. I earnestly pray for wisdom before I sit down to write my first sermon. All the years of teaching back home have led me to this point. I am comfortable in my element teaching clients in the gym, but I have never taught the Word of God, so this is a whole new curriculum to convey. I think to myself, "I am a fitness teacher by trade; however, I have never taught the Word of God. How hard can this be?" But because I have never attended one single class in seminary school, I feel like I am in unchartered territory.

As I sit down in the Crew Library during my break, I silently pray and start to write my very first sermon. I begin with an outline much like planning a lesson, and the message of course is always the same, the message of salvation. The Holy Spirit fills my mind and heart as my pen moves quickly on the paper and I flip through to the pages in the Bible that I am so familiar with from growing up. All those years in Sunday school and all those years watching my mother walk in faith are seeds deeply planted in my heart and mind. Talking about God is easy because I know the Word of God and I know His voice. I am not in unchartered territory as I thought; I am in familiar territory, as a child of God.

"The Spirit of the Sovereign Lord is on me"
(Isaiah 61:1 NIV).

I really want to call the pastors back home for some advice, but I know it is not realistic for me to have a long discussion with the difference in the time zones and the high cost of such a telephone call. The limited phone cards and phone lines available for the crew determine how much access to a telephone a person has during his or her break. I manage to finish writing my first sermon titled "God's Gift versus Our Gifts" within two hours as the words flowed quickly out of me and onto the paper (appendix 1). I am so eager and excited to share it with Brother Matthew on Saturday, the day before he disembarks on turnaround day.

I speak with Brother Matthew and meet him one last time. He lays his hand over my shoulder and prays for me. Tears run unceasingly down my cheeks as his words touch my heart. The presence of God overwhelms me and sends shivers from the crown of my head to the soles of my feet. I have never felt such a holy presence in my being, and I am moved beyond words. Tears run down my face as I feel restored, renewed in mind, and strengthened. I am filled with an anointing and fortitude that will enable me to be a minister for the crew onboard this ship for the remainder of my contract.

I have a new role and it is to walk as a prominent leader of faith for the crew. My heart is filled with a great sense of responsibility that I never felt back on land or at sea. Growing up in church back home, I was always behind the scenes volunteering in various capacities. I was often behind the piano or quietly stacking chairs or cleaning up after services. I was never at the front of the church leading in any capacity, let alone standing at the pulpit. Today God has directed my steps and led me to this point of public ministry. I wholeheartedly welcome the change in my walk. A verse comes to my mind from Luke 12:48 NIV: *"From everyone who has been given much, much will be demanded."* I am blessed beyond measure, and it is now time for me to give back since much is expected of me from this day forward.

I am ready for the challenge of added responsibilities and finally embrace the role to take over for Brother Matthew. I feel a sense of mission to accomplish. A newfound sense of purpose fills my heart, and, with every step I take in this journey, I pray for wisdom. The Holy Spirit sends me scripture verses throughout the day that pop up in my mind to encourage me: *"I will be with you"* (Exodus. 3:12 NIV).

Since Wednesday, when Brother Matthew spoke with me, word has spread like wildfire that I will be delivering the sermon to the crew on Sunday. Crew from all departments have heard that Lincee from the Entertainment Department is taking over for Brother Matthew. I did not dare tell my roommate or department colleagues that I am delivering the sermon today because I feel a bit of trepidation as to how my colleagues will take the news. They are always at the Crew Bar every night to party, smoke, and drink while tantalizing the sailors with their seductive dance moves.

After my shift at the end of the day, I quietly walk to my cabin and change out of my uniform. I put on a pair of black dress pants and a jacket over my blouse, also putting on some extra deodorant as I feel a bit nervous. I slap on some Chapstick and pack my bag with my large bottle of water, Bible, and sermon notes. As I walk down the i95 corridor on Deck Four to the back of the ship, many crew members turn their heads as I go past, surprised to see me dressed differently than usual. I have never dressed in such clean, formal attire with a touch of lip gloss. The crew all know that I am about to deliver my first sermon at the 11:00 p.m. church service held in the Staff Mess.

The crew in attendance is already physically tired and slouched in their seats at 11:30 p.m. when I finally stepped up to the pulpit. I deliver the sermon which lasts about thirty minutes. The crew have never heard me speak for more than three minutes. I captivate everyone's attention. Everyone in the room is hanging on to every word and scripture reference. As I speak from the pulpit, I see the crew members feverishly write each scripture verse down and flip through the Bible chapters for reference. Whether they are fascinated by my North American accent or the attire I am wearing, all their eyes are on me. Before I began, I had prayed that God would speak through me and the words of my mouth would touch their hearts and minds. I prayed that they would hear the message of salvation rather than see me behind the pulpit.

After the service is over, many crew members come up to me in tears to thank me for sharing the Word of God. They tell me they heard God speaking to them directly. Many tell me that they are excited to attend the Bible study on Wednesday to hear me speak again. "Glory to God!" I reply to each person when they shake my hand. "Praise the Lord!" they reply gleefully. Tonight, standing at the pulpit, is by far the best night of my life. I can feel the hand of God over me, the presence of the Holy Spirit speaking through me, and the love of God flowing through me to the crew members. This is the first time I have had such feelings and they are feelings I don't want to let go. I feel that my purpose and new-found ministry have unveiled themselves tonight, much to my own surprise. I am like an onion with another layer peeled back that I did not know existed within me. Before coming onto this cruise ship, my intention was to start a new chapter at thirty years of age and to explore life at sea. Today, I have learned this ministry is where God has delivered me. Much to my surprise, I know in my heart that I am in for an exciting journey ahead.

"No eye has seen, no ear has heard, no mind has conceived what God has prepared for those who love Him"
(1 Corinthians 2:9 NIV).

Since coming onboard, I have desperately wanted to find my purpose and to make some friends. My goal had been to explore my options and see what is available to me beyond my life back home. But, after this evening's church service, this renewed sense of purpose and peace changes my direction. Finding someone to befriend me during this contract no longer seems important. Searching for purpose on my own no longer seems to be a priority in this contract either. I remind myself as I walk back to my cabin that no eye can see, no ear can hear, nor any mind comprehend that which God has in store for me. I will walk in obedience, accepting the torch handed over to me by Brother Matthew, and I intend to walk in faith. I know in my heart that this new chapter of my life is going to be filled with much hope and adventure in the days ahead. I am beyond excited to see what will unfold for me during the remainder of this contract.

Chapter 6

The Noodle Man, Baker, and Milkshake Maker

When a man comes to like a sea life, he is not fit to live on land. Dr. Samuel Johnson

Today has been a long day and I have just finished working three shifts spread over thirteen hours entertaining passengers all over the ship in different stations hosting events. I felt so tired throughout the day that I did not even have energy to practice the piano in the chapel during my short breaks. I just want a hot shower and to lay in my bunk relaxing and watching television before drifting off to sleep. Walking back to my cabin, I decide to stop by my supervisor's cabin to ask for a small request; I would like a change in my work schedule so I can have my Wednesday and Sunday evening shifts end at 10:00 p.m. rather than 1:00 a.m.

Crew members across departments are, by large, friendly and cordial toward one another. They often have their cabin doors propped open, not only for air circulation, but because the tiny cabins feel somewhat claustrophobic. When I arrive at the doorstep of Peter's cabin, I see him at his desk eating a bowl of hot noodles while watching television. He looks up with noodles wrapped around his fork, about to take another bite, when he sees me smiling at his doorstep.

"Hi Lincee, what's up?" Peter asks as he bites into his forkful of noodles.

I immediately forget why I have come to his cabin and my eyes glean wide in surprise. "Peter, where in the world did you get hot noodles? It looks so delicious," I reply.

Generally, the Crew Mess on this ship close around 8:00 p.m. and the only food available at the end of the day is the day-old bread, leftover bruised fruit, and perhaps some stale rice and mystery meat that lay in pans. Sometimes, the leftover meals from the passenger dining room trickle down to the Crew Mess and it is a gamble to see if anything is appealing enough to eat. Most of the dining staff have first choice of the leftover passenger meals that have not been ordered off the menu. At the end of their shift, they carry off their dinner of leftover meals prepared in the galley. If the galley makes too much of a particular passenger menu item that hasn't been exhausted, then those dishes come down to the Crew Mess after 10:00 p.m. If a sailor does not have passenger deck privileges, this food is the only option to fill his or her hungry belly besides the alcohol in the Crew Bar. So, seeing Peter eat piping hot noodles in his cabin at 10:30 p.m. is something to be desired by anyone.

I have already left the passenger area and am down on Deck Four in the crew quarters, so the idea of going all the way back up to the top deck to the passenger buffet is not even a thought for me. I was not hungry when I left work, but as I stand at Peter's doorstep and smell the aroma of the hot noodles, suddenly I feel hungry.

"Lincee, if you are hungry, just call the noodle man and he will deliver noodles to you," Peter answered back.

"Noodle man? Who is the noodle man?" I ask with surprise.

"I don't know WHO he is. I just call him, and some random crew member delivers the noodles. Here is the number and it costs two dollars for noodles to be delivered to your cabin. If the sandwich man is busy, call the noodle man," Peter explains between chewing his noodles.

"Wow! I've never heard of the noodle man or the sandwich man. Is the sandwich man the same guy from passenger room service?"

"Yes, it's the same guy but the delivery guy changes every time, so be careful with the contraband as you don't want to be caught," Peter quietly answers back in a hushed voice. He next asks, "Hey, did you want something?" which reminds me of why I purposely stopped by his cabin.

We discuss the work schedule for a bit and then I head back to my cabin, now feeling very hungry at 11:00 p.m. I enter my quarters to find Katerina already in her bunk watching television.

"Hey, Katerina, guess what I learned tonight? There is a noodle man onboard that delivers hot noodles! Just like the sandwich man!" I excitedly tell my roommate.

"Let's order hot noodles!" Katerina replies as she sits up from her bed. We both agree, so we rummage through our purses for two single one-dollar bills to pay for the noodles. I call the number Peter gave me and within ten minutes two piping hot bowls of noodles arrive at our door hidden inside a large, white paper laundry bag. It is beyond belief to have two bowls of contraband delivered to fill our hungry bellies at the cost two American dollars each.

For just a very brief moment, I feel a sense of guilt and sin because I have engaged in an illegal activity. I paid for food that was not supposed to be available for crew at this hour of the day. Where did the food come from? I do not care. How did the food get cooked? I do not care. Who got to keep the money? I do not care. Someone just risked their job delivering contraband to my cabin and, for the second time, I am engaged in the underground criminal activity known as the black market amongst crew members. Now I have the number to the sandwich man and the noodle man. The person who takes the call and order is not the same crew member who prepares the food or who delivers it. I never get to know the face of the person with whom I place my order or the person who cooks the food, but those crew members now know my cabin number, my name, and my desire for delicious contraband. Contraband at sea is an underground market of trading goods and services that I have never thought to be of any coveted importance until I was deprived of such comforts, desires, and needs. On land, life is quite different as I always have the means to purchase what I need or to complete simple tasks, like make a telephone call or have enough soap to do laundry. Purchasing items at a grocery store or pharmacy is a relatively simple and mundane task, and I always have had the required funds to pay for the goods either in cash or with my credit card. Such simplicities and basics of life can be taken for granted and a comfortable living environment may not be appreciated until it is all slowly taken away from you.

At sea, the most coveted yet most scarce commodity for a sailor is a sound sleep. After a while, without sleep, one cannot function. The mind and body are constantly assaulted with various things that, over a period of time, become just unbearable and dreadful enough to drive any soul mad. Constant noises that you can't control invade your cabin and rob you of sleep, such as the creaking steel sounds that become more apparent with every swell of the sea or the blaring music from your neighbour's cabin down the hall. All throughout the day, the crew members are on different scheduled breaks and one's cabin is the only escape and reprieve from the demanding passengers. The loud cackles of voices, be it laughter, chatter, debates, or loud television channels in different languages, all infiltrate the long corridors below deck and into your cabin, stealing from you any quiet downtime or sleep. Headphones are not enough to drown out any noises as the walls between the cabins are paper thin, and, if your cabin is against the hull of the ship as my cabin is, you can hear the water splashing up against your bed every night.

Many nights I pray that our ship will not hit an iceberg or whale, things that could tear a hole right into my cabin. Yet nightly, every few hours, a loud bang against the cold steel wall wakes me up from my sleep. Often times, the ship lists and tilts so far to the port or starboard side that I either roll right into the cold, steel cabin wall or up against the bed rail that saves me from falling down to the floor from my top bunk.

Another issue to contend with are the built-in vents and fans that are fixed on the crew cabins' ceilings. In each cabin, the airflow is controlled by the central heating system, and it circulates poor air quality below decks. Yet, it forcefully pushes out cold air that makes me shiver under my blankets under the loud ceiling fan. Aside from these constant physical assaults, it is the cold temperature in the cabins below the waterline that no one can control. Cabins below deck are often a few degrees lower in temperature than the passenger cabins above the water line. Every night, I wear a zippered sweater over my pajamas with its hood over my head and I still shiver under my blankets. These constant noises, the ship's motions of swaying back and forth either from bow to stern or portside to starboard side, and the cold temperature are more than enough to contend with for any sailor.

Moreover, on top of such challenges for a sailor, the ship's smells are enough to make one want to vomit if you stay in the corridors too long. The stench of every sailor's shoes propped up against the walls outside every cabin door makes for an aroma wafting down the hallways that would kill a skunk. Along the maze of corridors below passenger decks, the crew members are surrounded by watertight doors between each zone and there is also the constant clanging of the steel garbage and recycling bins that are bolted down by rope beside each of these doors. Against the thin cabin walls, they make for a rhythm that keeps in time with the ship's motion as swinging lids hit against the railing with every swell of the ship.

Every time the ship is in rough waters, the ship's alarm bells go off to warn crew that the watertight doors are about to close. The bells ring over a certain period at a pitch that pierces the ears with a deafening volume to announce that the doors are quickly closing. If you don't steer clear in time for their closing, you can die, literally sliced in half, or lose a limb as in the case of one crew member who tried to jump through the divider before the door closed.

This man's shirt got caught on the handle and he did not pull it out it time. The watertight door closed and amputated his arm right from his body while he watched in horror. His blood poured out and splattered all over the walls and floor of the corridor as he looked at his missing arm and stood in a pool of his own blood. His agonizing screams of tortured pain reached every cabin door with terror throughout three zones. Emergency personnel were notified, and the Captain's immediate announcement came over the entire ship. "Tango! Tango! Tango! Deck Three, Zone Two portside! Tango! Stretcher party immediately!" When the entire crew heard this announcement throughout the ship, it was heartbreak as we knew someone had just lost a limb in the crew quarters.

When the Captain's announcements come on to reveal certain incidences through codes, we know imminent danger, compromised safety, or an emergency is taking place. Though the passengers do not know what these codes mean, it is a silent message for crew to be informed of such critical matters. When the ship's bells ring for a certain duration, it alerts the crew of an emergency unfolding. Crew members then drop everything, wherever they are on the ship, and immediately go to their cabins to retrieve their life jackets and proceed to their emergency muster stations for duty. When I first heard the bells, I recall the passengers' looks of concern when all service immediately ceased and the crew stopped what they were doing, turned away from the passengers without another word, quickly scurried to the nearest crew exit door, and disappeared, leaving all the passengers to wonder what was going on or what was about to happen.

The atmosphere is quite eerie in the passenger areas without a single crew member. Panic starts to spread amongst the passengers when the crew alert signal is broadcast without a Captain's announcement to immediately explain what is happening. When such bells go off to alert the crew, we are not to even stop and answer the passengers' questions. Within minutes of the crew alert signal, and once the crew are in position, then the passengers are notified with an announcement from the Captain as to how to proceed in the next few moments.

On this day, there is an announcement from the Bridge that shocks the crew. As a crew member, there are just some announcements from the Captain we never want to hear. Aside from Code Tango, there are several other codes that make the crew fear for their lives. Today, just as the ship is pulling into port to be aligned by the pier, a surprise Code Oscar announcement makes every crew member's heart skip a beat. Our ship is about six feet in distance from the pier and the thrusters on the portside are pushing the ship to dock on the starboard side. The Captain and officers are on the starboard side of the Bridge wing, watching below as the adjoining Pilot on the Bridge assists the Captain in docking and aligning the ship. Suddenly, a man in white trousers, white shirt, and black shoes jumps over the railing of the open Deck Seven that wraps around the entire ship. He tries to jump onto the pier which is still about six feet from the starboard side of the railing and about thirty feet below. Immediately, the Captain makes the following announcement, urgently broadcasting over the entire ship with a stern and loud voice, "Oscar! Oscar! Oscar! Deck Seven, Starboard side, Zone Three! Oscar!"

The crew throughout the entire ship stop for a moment and look at one another with eyes wide open, holding back a surreptitious fear so as not to alarm the passengers of our growing concern. A number of questions run through the mind of the crew members: What type of Code Oscar is this incident? Does it involve a passenger? A crew member? Is there bloodshed? Was it intentional or an accident? So many questions and concerns run through a sailor's mind with just that one word "OSCAR." It's heartbreak to hear of any death that may occur in the moments that may follow.

Pier-side authorities are waiting as normal, lined up along the pier, for the ship to dock. About twenty men in total stand alongside the pier patiently waiting for the mooring ropes to be released so the ship can be tied up on the bollards along the pier. All the men on the pier watch in shocked horror as they see the man jump from the ship. Why couldn't he wait for the ship to dock? Is he a passenger who is tired of the long lines to get off the gangway? Or is it a passenger who wants to get an early start on the sales in the shops along the shoreside? Several of the crew in the Security Department immediately proceed to Deck Seven starboard side just moments after the man has jumped and the Captain has made his announcement.

All the passengers and crew members on Deck Seven lean over the railing in shock watching the man. He almost landed on the pier, but now hangs with his legs dangling off its edge. He tries to desperately pull himself up onto the hard asphalt as the shoreside security and personnel run to his aid to pull him up. The Captain and Bridge Officers, along with everyone watching, hold their breath, hoping the man's legs are not going to be severed by the steel tonnage of the ship. Everyone watches in horror as the moments unfold while the Bridge Officers and Captain are frozen in place on the starboard wing of the Bridge, watching in urgency in a state of helplessness. The mega-ton steel ship barely misses the man's legs by a few seconds as he is pulled up to the pier and retained.

The Captain, with radio in hand on the Bridge, is listening to SECO, who is the Chief Security Officer onboard. He is on Deck Seven shouting directions to the security personnel on the pier. Shoreside security pulls the man up, and, to everyone's dismay, his clothing indicates he is a crew member from the galley. He is the Russian Chief Baker, named Vladimir, who joined the ship about three weeks ago. Chefs and cooks in the galley do not wear a name badge with pins as it may fall into the food preparations, instead their name is sewn onto the uniform. This Russian Baker is barely standing up on the pier with several men holding him and retaining him from fleeing any further. He is bleeding at the knee and a portion of his uniform is ripped from the jump. Everyone breathes a sigh of relief that he still has his legs attached to his body. However, this security incident is far from over.

As soon as the ship pulls alongside the pier, the Captain radios the SECO to bring the crew member to the Medical Centre escorted by several security personnel. The crew members in the Deck Department immediately clear the gangway area where passengers are lined up waiting to disembark, and then close the doors to prevent the passengers from seeing what has unfolded with Vladimir. As the shell door opens on the side of the ship, the Deck Department sets up the gangway. By this time, the entire medical staff, which includes the Senior Doctor, Doctor, and Nurse, stand ready with the stretcher to retrieve our injured crew member. As soon as the gangway is secured, the medical team heads down it, swiftly moving with stretcher in tow and the medical bag. After a quick assessment by the Senior Doctor, the medical team places Vladimir on the stretcher to bring him to the Medical Centre under the escort of onboard security.

This incident holds up the passenger disembarkation process for about twenty minutes as everyone tries to quickly usher the ailing Russian crew member to the Medical Centre. The security personnel guide the entire medical team quickly from Zone Two to Zone Three, moving aside any oncoming crew traffic along the i95 on Deck Four. Security personnel stands by Vladimir the whole time in the Medical Centre as doctors and nurses tend to him. Security needs to ensure the Chief Baker will not try to escape again, even with his injured knee. The Doctor tries to calm him down, but Vladimir is speaking in Russian, rather than in English. Every crew member must speak English in order to be hired for any cruise line, even if they work behind the scenes in the galley where they never have any contact with passengers. English is always the required spoken language in passenger areas and a requirement in the crew areas when on duty. After what seems like a long time, Vladimir finally calms down to be assessed and treated for his injured knee. However, the systemic issues that caused him to jump and run are much deeper and cannot be fixed by any doctor or nurse onboard. It is now time for the SECO to sit down with Vladimir to investigate the cause of the intended escape. Calmly, the SECO sits with the Doctor to begin his investigation and report.

Vladimir is the Chief Baker in charge of all the cookies. Onboard the ship on this itinerary in the Caribbean, there are 2,600 passengers and 1,300 crew members but only one Chief Baker of cookies in the galley. Recently, the Head Office made the decision for all ships across the fleet of fifteen that every passenger will receive two cookies on a plate with chocolates at the end of the day when the cabin stewards turn down the bed and refresh the towels. Normally, cabin stewards only place chocolates on the pillow, but the new directive from the Head Office means that Vladimir is to bake a minimum total of 5,200 cookies every night. Someone up at the Head Office came up with this brilliant idea and wanted a trial test to see if it would improve the ratings from the passengers. Also, it is an idea to set this cruise line apart from the competition. The last thing a passenger will remember before going to sleep is to see, and hopefully eat, the two cookies and chocolates placed by the bedside night table and, in turn, give the cruise a better rating.

Vladimir's responsibilities require him to bake the minimum required 5,200 passenger cookies by 5:00 p.m. which must be distributed to the cabin stewards for pickup by 6:00 p.m. He also must bake enough cookies for the buffets located around the ship during breakfast, morning, and evening serving times. In addition, he also needs to bake cookies for the dining rooms' dessert menu, cookies for teatime, cookies for the youth program, and cookies for the deck parties. These are the total daily required cookies for the passengers. Then, Vladimir also must bake cookies for the crew, staff, and officer messes, and for the Bridge Officers every day. Roughly, that is about another one thousand cookies on top of the 5,200 bedtime cookies that must come from Vladimir on time and in perfect condition. Vladimir is a professional baker back home in Russia. He is a reputable, established, and experienced baker with a good home life. He came onboard this luxury cruise ship to share his joy and love of baking with the world. The salary in American dollars is lucrative enough to lure him away from all his comforts back home and to leave his family and try an adventure at sea. Vladimir did not know that he would be baking fifteen hours every day and pumping out over six thousand cookies daily.

Vladimir has no sunshine, no fresh air, no time to go ashore to explore, no time to make friends, and no opportunities to engage with other crew members. He wakes up and bakes nonstop, and with the short breaks he does have, he eats, showers, and tries to sleep well. But with all the sleep deprivations and sensory overload due to the constant noises, ship movements, poor air quality, and limited selection of food for the crew, it finally takes its toll on Vladimir's mental state. What soul can handle such a demanding and heavy workload coupled with stress and deprivations? For a sound state of mind, every person needs fresh air, sunshine, quality rest, food, and sleep. One does not realize how priceless such luxuries are in life until they are slowly taken away, bit by bit, under harsh working and living conditions. Vladimir had gone mad and was sick of cookies. He desperately wanted fresh air, sunshine, and a taste of some freedom which led him this morning to walk from the galley below deck up to Deck Seven and jump from the ship. There is no medicine to cure the mind of this baker, except to give him what his mental state hungers for—the necessities of life.

The security incident report is now complete and is sent to the Captain who will review it before it goes to the Head Office. The Doctor makes the executive decision that this crew member be immediately sent home on psychiatric grounds, which means he is not fired. He will get an escort to deliver him directly to his home country to ensure his safe arrival to his doorstep. After this incident, Head Office swiftly makes the decision to discontinue sending two cookies to every passenger at turndown time.

News spreads like wildfire throughout the departments involved regarding the cookies. Now the galley dishwashers are relieved to have to wash 2,600 less dishes. The cabin stewards are relieved to not have to start their shift fifteen minutes earlier to count and collect cookies for their section. The cleaning staff are pleased they do not have to vacuum up cookie crumbs along the corridors, and the bakers in the galley are delighted that the aroma of cookies will not overtake the entire galley in that zone. Everyone is sick of cookies and the Head Office knew no better. The passenger rating scores showed no difference at all for those three weeks. Fewer cookies mean less expense for ingredients and less stress for everyone involved. It is the end of the cookie initiative across the entire fleet of fifteen ships. Vladimir goes home at the next port of call as soon as the flights are arranged. He never comes back to sea.

Whenever the seas are rough, the Accommodation Department takes out small, white barf bags that are lined inside with stiff wax paper and places them around the ship's common passenger areas, like the elevators. These barf bags are about the size of a small brown paper bag and so they are the perfect mode of hidden transport for contraband amongst the crew. One can fit a sandwich from the passenger buffet inside the bag or a few cookies to store for later in your cabin when you are hungry after your shift. Whenever the bags come out for the passengers, crew members take them and hide them in their shoulder bags for later use.

One day, as I was walking along deck, I pass by the ice cream parlour and see a sign that they have milkshakes for sale. I walk up to the ice cream counter when no passengers are around and ask the girl behind it about the milkshakes. She reminds me that milkshakes are only sold to passengers and that crew with deck privileges can only have ice cream. The Mexican girl sees the dismayed look on my face and continues in her thick accent, "Since you have deck privileges and can eat at the passenger's buffet, can you get me a guacamole sandwich? I will trade you for a milkshake."

My eyes light up and I reply, "Sounds like a perfect trade. I will go back to the buffet and deliver you a sandwich. I will be right back."

The crew members who serve food to the passengers do not have deck privileges to eat the food they serve nor to walk in passenger areas. The crew must use dedicated crew elevators and crew stairs to get to their workstations. Because I am of a higher rank in the Entertainment Department, I have deck privileges. I can walk anywhere in the passenger areas in my uniform and I can eat anywhere on the ship, except the formal passenger dining rooms. Suddenly, I really want a milkshake and my mission now is to deliver the goods to this Mexican girl. She must have been craving some real passenger food for quite some time.

I walk back to the buffet and carefully take a large plate and pack on several sandwiches with guacamole and a variety of cookies. I unassumingly carry my full plate of food to the back of the ship where there are fewer passengers and traffic. I sit down at a table in the corner and, when no one is watching, I carefully open the first white barf bag I keep inside my large shoulder bag. I wrapped the sandwich in a napkin, place it in the barf bag, and seal it up inside my large purse. I reach inside my purse and open another white barf bag, surreptitiously take another sandwich off my plate, wrap it inside another napkin and put it inside my purse which has the white bag open and ready. In the third barf bag, I place all the cookies inside. Now my purse is packed with three barf bags filled to the rim with contraband. I take my large water bottle out of my purse to make space for the contraband to fit loosely. Within two minutes, my entire plate of food is empty. I get up and start to walk back to Zone Three towards the middle of the ship to deliver the goods.

As I approach the ice cream parlour, the girl looks at me as she is serving passengers and nods towards the back. I walk towards the door beside the ice cream parlour labeled "Crew Only" and pull it open. I step inside to see there is another door to the right that opens to the ice cream parlor and ahead of me is an elevator for the crew. I look up at the ceiling and see no cameras. This is a safe place, hidden from cameras and passengers, for the contraband exchange. After she serves the passengers, she makes a milkshake for me and brings it to the back. A huge smile brightens her face as I take out three white bags of sandwiches and cookies. She gives me the milkshake and for a few moments we both just look at each other in silence and delight.

"I haven't had a sandwich with guacamole for months since I joined this ship. I really needed some real food. Thank you so much! I am so happy!" Maria tells me.

"Thank you so much for the milkshake. Whenever you want passenger food, just let me know, and I can get it for you. Here is my pager number," I cheerfully reply back.

Maria answers back, "Lincee, you got me TWO sandwiches? Wow, I am so happy! Thank you so much. Anytime you want a milkshake, just come through the back door when I am working."

"Okay, thanks, Maria." I answer back.

Maria hides the white bags in her purse and goes back to serving the passengers. I stand alone to quickly finish my milkshake between the two crew doors because I cannot carry this milkshake in passenger or crew quarters to enjoy in my cabin as it is forbidden for crew to drink a milkshake meant only for passengers. Nor are we permitted to store any perishable food in the crew cabins. Within a few minutes, I finish the entire milkshake and leave the glass in the back pantry of the ice cream parlour. I walk down the corridor towards the crew elevator. Honestly, I feel bad that certain crew members are not permitted to eat a better selection and quality of food which I understand is because of the ranks and status at sea.

It really is unfortunate that the Crew Mess does not have a more varied menu; it is the same menu week after week, month after month, which becomes incredibly bland and boring very quickly. I feel like I helped Maria a little bit by giving her some sort of access to better quality food and that I made her day. In my heart, I feel I like I have done a good deed. However, in my mind, I know I just did something incredibly wrong and against the ship's rules. I engaged once again in the underground black market of trading goods illegally and without any consequence. Yet the trade was a mutual agreement between two parties. The trade did not cost the company any loss in revenue, and the trade was of equal value, so no one was at a loss or sacrifice. Is this a sin? I wrestle with this thought as I ride down the elevator. Not at all! I convince myself that I am like Robin Hood who is taking food from the passengers to give the crew. No harm in that, right? Rather than making the crew wait for passenger leftovers to be brought down to the Crew Mess at the end of the day, I just expedited the process. I am Robin Hood to the rescue!

Chapter 7

Drug Mule

We are tied to the ocean. And when we go back to the sea,
whether it is to sail or to watch – we are going back from
whence we came. John F. Kennedy

t is another glorious, sunny day as this beautiful luxury cruise ship sails through the Caribbean waters. This vessel carries 2,800 passengers and 1,300 crew members of all nationalities. Working on this larger vessel with a different route brings another type of excitement and adventure that cannot be paralleled to anything on land. I am so excited to be back at sea for another interesting contract with a new itinerary and new roommate. The moment I step foot on the gangway, I forget all about my life on land. I am so excited to be exploring another part of the world with a whole slew of new crew mates to befriend. After my last contract in Alaska on the smaller ship, I stayed on land for about ten months before I had the itch to return to sea for another adventure. Teaching clients at the gym became extremely boring and it was the same routine every day, so I was ready for a change in scenery. I gladly welcomed another contract to do something different.

After a week of sailing around the Caribbean, I quickly settle into the routine as the same repeating itinerary will unfold for the next eight weeks. Our ship left Jamaica last night and is scheduled to dock at St. Thomas at 8:00 a.m., and I am excited to have the day off in St. Thomas. I am not scheduled to work again till 7:00 p.m. when the ship sails. Normally I sleep in when I have the day off. This morning, however, I wake up rather hungry after spending the night in my boyfriend's cabin.

I am so glad to have started off this contract meeting Anthony at the crew hotel on the morning of joining the ship last week. I was coming down the escalator of the hotel at 6:00 a.m. to check out when I saw all the crew members waiting in the lobby for the cruise ship bus to pick us up. Little did I know that all the crew members in the hotel lobby already had their eyes on this unsuspecting crew member as I was the only female in the entire lobby of about one hundred men awaiting the two crew buses to arrive. After handing in my hotel key, I stepped outside the front door of the hotel for some fresh air with my luggage in tow and up came this handsome fellow to stand beside me as I waited for the bus.

I noticed the fellow standing beside me didn't have any luggage with him, so I figured he was just a tourist visiting and not joining the ship. We exchanged pleasantries and I quickly learned he too was waiting for the same bus to join the ship. "Where is your luggage? You have a ten-month contract and no luggage?" I asked in surprise. Anthony replied, "The airline lost all my luggage and I didn't even pack a good carry-on, so I don't even have a toothbrush!" I kindly suggested, "You must always pack smart and bring a good carry-on with all the basic necessities as you know that even passengers lose their luggage. How can you afford to take the risk of ten months without underwear?" My contract is only three months and I had packed twenty pieces of underwear due to the limited time to do laundry plus the limited facilities.

I felt really bad for Anthony, so I offered to assist him when we boarded the ship to access the basic necessities until his luggage arrived, if it ever did. I was glad to have made a friend before I even stepped foot on the ship since I know this contract will be harder for me to make friends with a larger amount of crew on the manifest. We continued our conversation as we boarded the crew bus ride to join the ship.

I roll out of bed delighted that Anthony is now my boyfriend. I give him a quick kiss, get dressed, and go back to my own cabin to prepare for my day and head to the mess for a quick breakfast. I walk to the back of the ship towards the Crew Mess to dine because the Staff Mess closes at 9:00 a.m. and the Crew Mess is open all day. I pick up a tray and start walking through the buffet line of breakfast foods. I slide my tray along the counter as I pick up the ladles to fill my plate with eggs, bacon, and some toast. Suddenly, the Captain comes on the speaker to make an announcement which all the crew members are expecting. An announcement from the Captain occurs every time shortly after we dock in port. When all the passengers have disembarked for their tours and are ashore, the Captain comes on about one and half hours later and grants "Crew Shore Leave." This announcement means all crew can now approach the gangway and go ashore unless one has In-Port-Manning, or IPM, duties that day. However, this Captain's announcement comes as a shock to the entire crew of 1,300 members, and most especially to me.

"Attention! Attention! Crew member Lincee Tang, Supernumerary number S68, report immediately to the Crew Bar Deck Eight Forward. I repeat, crew member Lincee Tang, number S68, report to the Crew Bar Deck Eight Forward immediately." The Captain forcefully speaks in succinct, rhythmic, broken syllables to ensure his thick Italian accent will not be misunderstood and that I get the clear message to immediately report to the required point of reference.

As soon as I hear this announcement, I freeze in the Crew Mess, holding my food tray tightly with both hands. I look up and every crew member in the mess is staring at me. There are about one hundred crew members eating breakfast at the dining tables behind me and they all look up to see me frozen in shock at the buffet line. No other announcement follows about granting crew shore leave. Everyone is eagerly anticipating the next announcement from the Captain, but none comes. It is time for me to move, and fast, in response to the Captain's announcement.

I immediately leave the food tray on the buffet line and head toward the exit. The staff member behind the buffet line yells at me, "Hey, you can't leave your tray of food here!"

"I'll be back. I want to eat breakfast, but the Captain just called for me. I WILL be back!" I yell as I rush out of the Crew Mess.

This mess is at the back of the ship in Zone Five and the Crew Bar is located all the way in the front of the ship in Zone One. Walking this distance is going to take me at least ten minutes, if not more. The walk from stern to bow and from Deck Four to Deck Eight is a total of five zones to navigate through. At this point, I start to panic and wonder why in the world would the Captain make such an announcement looking for me. He broadcasted his announcement not only in crew quarters, but over the entire ship which means there must be a search warrant for me, and that no security personnel could find me. As I quickly pick up my pace, I realize the reason why no one could find me was because I slept in Anthony's cabin last night and I did not have my pager on me. Well, I was off duty as of 10:00 p.m. last night and had no reason to carry my pager until I went on duty again at 7:00 p.m. today. I know I didn't do anything wrong. I know I am clean from any criminal activity, so why is the Captain looking for me?

At this point it is almost 9:30 a.m. and the Captain has not come back on to make the announcement to grant crew shore leave. It has already been ninety minutes since the ship has docked and it is overdue for crew shore leave to be granted. This means the entire crew of 1,300 people are anxiously waiting around the entire ship, many standing by the gangways to be granted permission to go ashore, all wondering what or who in the world is keeping the Captain from making the announcement. It is me! I am holding up the Captain and he is holding the entire crew onboard as hostage for a reason unbeknownst to me. After thirteen minutes of rushing from stern to bow, I finally reach Deck Eight Forward at the entrance to the Crew Bar. I arrive huffing and puffing as I rush toward the glass doors.

As soon as I turn the corner, I see two crew Security Officers and two shoreside police officers along with a sniffing dog all looking at me. The SECO and other crew security look straight at me with serious faces and wide eyes. The SECO escorts me through the glass doors to enter the Crew Bar where there are more shoreside policemen, policewomen, and police dogs from St. Thomas. I finally catch my breath, and as soon as I step inside, I see all eyes on me. Approximately two hundred crew members are lined up against the wall. I immediately notice there are three groups of crew members sectioned off. All the Mexicans are in one group, all the Russians are in another group, and all the Black crew members are grouped together. I have no idea what is happening or about to unfold, but when I see all the crew members stare at me in silence, I start to panic. I do not fit into any of these three groups. I am the only female, the only North American, and the only crew member in my department that has been summoned. "What in the world is going on?" I think to myself in dismay.

The first person to step forward is my short Filipino supervisor of five feet, and she is the first to speak in her thick accent with a fierce look of anger on her face. "Where have you been, Lincee? What took you so long to get here since the Captain's announcement?" she demands loud enough for everyone to hear. A hushed silence falls over the entire crew as everyone leans in eagerly anticipating my answer as to the holdup of the Captain granting crew shore leave.

I calmly answer my supervisor as I stand tall at five feet nine inches, looking fiercely down at her, "I was in the Crew Mess getting some breakfast to eat. I came as soon as I heard the Captain's announcement. It takes time to walk from Zone Five to Zone One. Why was I called here?"

Every officer and the gathered crew stand in silence listening to my explanation for my delay in arriving. I look over the shoulder of my supervisor to take in the crew members again and I see my boyfriend standing in the group with all the other Black crew members. Most of the crew members in that group are from the Caribbean and the rest are from Africa, Mauritius, and Europe. I know all the Black crew members as they are my friends and they spend time with my boyfriend and me. I don't know any of the people in the other two groups of crew members who are sectioned off. I am still wondering why all these two hundred crew members are on the other side of the room and why I have been called here standing on this side with all the officers. I really do not know how I fit into this picture.

"Lincee, why didn't you answer your pager? Security has been searching for you since the authorities came onboard and you have been declared a missing crew member. That's why we had to call the Captain to make that announcement!" My supervisor sternly wags her finger at me in anger. Immediately, a shoreside policeman stands up and speaks very sternly to me.

"You have been called here because we have reason to believe you need a drug test. Fill this cup right now," he loudly directs as he thrusts the clear plastic container at me.

Suddenly, it dawns on me why I was called and why all these specific crew members of these nationalities were called here too. They suspect us to be drug mules, transporting or using drugs. Anger starts to rise in me as I look back at the police officer. How dare they call upon all the Mexicans, Russians, and Black crew members, blatantly discriminating us and suspecting us of being drug mules? How in the world do I fit into all of this? There isn't one single North American or woman standing in any of the three groups, and here I am being interrogated and told what to do.

I forcefully answer back in my firm voice, loud enough for every person to hear me. "Excuse me?" I say, my eyes wide open, "I am North American, and I know my rights. I will NOT be interrogated nor will I be told to fill that cup!" I stop here because I know I cannot ask for a lawyer nor do I have any rights. I am at sea and all these crew members have been already drug tested and interrogated. I am the final one who needs to be tested so I am holding everyone up. All two hundred crew members in front of me are clean and I am the last to be tested as drugs still have not been found onboard. Immediately, my supervisor steps in, "Lincee, fill the cup now, everyone is waiting." She looks at me with pleading eyes.

I loudly answer back, "I cannot fill the cup because my bladder is empty. I emptied it when I woke up, and I was just about to eat breakfast in the Crew Mess when the Captain called, so even my stomach is empty."

A police officer directs the crew security officers to fetch me several glasses of water. My supervisor continues, "Lincee, why didn't you carry your pager? I paged you and you did not answer. We went to your cabin and your bed was not slept in. Where have you been?" The entire Crew Bar falls silent as she peppers me with all these questions. Everyone wants to know the answers and so do the police.

I am angry at this point because my supervisor has just insinuated that I was sleeping elsewhere and has assumed I did not do my due diligence and carry my pager as required when I am on duty. My reputation has been tarnished within a matter of ten seconds when she spoke loudly enough for everyone to hear. The security personnel bring over three glasses of water and place them on the table in front of the shoreside officers. One officer points to the glasses, looks at me, and says firmly, "DRINK!"

At this point, I know it will take at least twenty minutes for me to drink all this water and for it to pass through to my bladder. I calmly walk toward the table and pick up the first glass of water and take a gulp. Every single person in the Crew Bar has their eyes fixed on me as do all the officers in uniform. My supervisor is waiting for my answers, and the crew members want to see how I will respond to her in front of all these police officers. I have the platform now and, with glass in hand, I pause, turn around, and face my supervisor. A hush of silence ripples throughout the entire room.

The North American in me is fierce as I turn to answer her interrogating questions that have embarrassed the hell out of me. In my firm, loud voice I retort back, looking down on her. "How DARE you question my whereabouts on my personal down time! Where I sleep is NONE of YOUR business or ANYONE's business. I am not obligated to inform you what I do during my off time. When I am at work, I report to you. When I am off work, it is my personal time and I am in no way, shape, or form obligated to divulge such information to you regarding my conduct." I pause to take another drink from my glass and realize that my Scottish accent slipped out a bit within my North American accent when I am upset.

Quiet shock ripples through all the crew members and all the officers. Everyone cannot believe what has come out of my mouth and how I sternly spoke back to my superior.

The atmosphere is tense and as thick as fog. Not a sound can be heard after my last words. I continue looking straight down at my supervisor's face which is now beet red with anger. "Furthermore, I am not obligated to carry my pager when I am off duty. I finished my duty at 10:00 p.m. last night and am not on duty again till 7:00 p.m. tonight and, according to my contract, I do not have to carry my pager when I am off duty." I finish off the first glass of water and walk over to the table, firmly placing the empty glass down and picking up another one. I drink the entire glass.

My supervisor stands in shock as she has never had any staff member speak to her or stand up for themselves in such a manner, and she does not know how to reply. Crew members generally never speak back to their supervisors, even when they are in the wrong. Yet the North American in me knows I am accurate regarding my contract duties and carrying the pager. My supervisor knows that I know my rights, the policies, and the procedures, and that she cannot demand or has the right to make me answer her questions.

Finished with my second glass of water, I place it on the table. I pause for a brief moment as I pick up the third glass. I feel all eyes on me as I pick up this last glass. I turn to walk towards the three groups of crew members standing patiently waiting for me to drink it and then fill the plastic container with my urine. Every crew member standing in the Crew Bar knows the results of my drug test determine whether the Captain will grant shore leave for the entire crew. However, the remaining one thousand crew members around the ship have no idea what the reason is for the hold-up is, except they all know WHO is holding up the Captain's announcement; it is a crew member named Lincee, Supernumerary number S68, who the Captain had summoned.

As I stare into the crowd of crew members with glass in hand, I look at my boyfriend and we make eye contact. I don't want to give him away to the police. However, every crew member in the room already knows that I am the girl-friend of one of the crew members standing in the group of Black staff. I am sure just about everyone here thinks I am the ideal unsuspected drug mule in some underground drug trade from Jamaica to St. Thomas for this drug test to be required. In their opinion, it is just a matter of time when the truth comes to light. The atmosphere grows more intense at the clock ticks. Not a sound is heard but silence as all the sailors stare at me while I drink the last glass of water. I turn around and put the glass back on the table. My belly is full of water and it will take some time for it to get to my bladder. Time is ticking and my supervisor looks at her watch and tells me, "Lincee, it's almost ten o'clock."

"It will take a bit more time for the water to get from my belly to my bladder," I reply.

The ship security and police officers, two hundred crew members, and my supervisor stare at me, even the dog! I can assure you that staring at a person will not make water move any faster from her belly to her bladder. It is now my turn to question the officers. From the moment I stepped into this Crew Bar, I have been peppered nonstop with questions. I have the platform now and I have them all waiting for my next move to fill that pee cup for the drug test. I choose my words with fastidious care to ensure I am clearly understood. I continue to speak firmly in my strong-willed voice, "Why are there no Asian crew members here for the drug test? Approximately eighty percent of the crew are Asians. Why am I singled out as the only female crew member being tested?"

All the officers stare back at me not knowing how to answer my questions; they look at one another not knowing even who should answer my questions. No one is obligated to answer me, however, every crew member in these three groups also want to know the answers. The evidence is overwhelmingly clear; it is pure, blatant discrimination. Only the Mexican, Russian, and Black crew members have been summoned for drug testing as well as me who does not fit into any of these categories. Of the 1,300 crew members onboard this ship, approximately 900 are from the Philippines. Aside from the Filipino, other Asian crew members, and Europeans, just about all the other nationalities of crew members are here in the Crew Bar being drug tested.

I already know the answers to my questions, but I want to hear it from these shoreside police officers so every crew member present can hear this discrimination loud and clear. I am now told about the rules and expectations of this surprise random drug test. Our ship was in international waters when it left Jamaica, but once it reached about twenty-four miles outside the shoreside of St. Thomas, our ship was sailing in American waters. I am now informed about the rules and the laws pertaining to being at sea. The law is now American, the rules are American, and the drug test is American. Despite the ship not sailing under the America flag, a ship follows the rules of the flag it sails under when in international waters. The headquarters and offices of this cruise company are located in America, yet the law is not American until the ship is in American waters. This cruise company sails under the flag of another country and follows the rules of that country. I think to myself, am I hearing this correctly?

The officers facing me now are upholding American laws and rights in their conduct. Being a North American does not hold any weight when I am on the ship. Whichever passport you carry does not matter when you are in international waters. You have limited rights and few laws to protect you when you are on international waters. No country wants to be accountable for your actions when you are on international water nor does any country want to deal with you if you commit a crime at sea. Yet, as soon as the ship hit American waters, only an American passport holds any weight.

The policewoman from St. Thomas picks up the clear plastic pee container and hands it to me. "Fill it now!" she speaks authoritatively towards me. I take the cup from her and quietly reply, "I will try." I start to walk towards the ladies' washroom, and she is right behind me. "I will escort you to the washroom and I will need to watch you fill the cup." I immediately turn around and stop. I see to my left all those male crew members watching my every move and waiting for my response to the policewoman.

"Excuse me? No thank you! I do not need you to watch me fill this cup. I will fill the cup in privacy," I reply in my loud and firm voice.

"I need to see that it is you that fills this cup and no other person." She tries to usher me into the washroom.

I stand my ground and do not budge or turn. She looks at me and all the crew members are watching and listening in shock as this conversation unfolds.

She finally concedes, "Okay, I do not have to watch you, but let me check to see that no other person is in the washroom with you when you fill this cup. I need the washroom door open and the stall door open so I can hear you fill the cup."

I slowly turn around and head towards the women's washroom. She props open the door and checks the stalls which are all empty. I enter the first stall and leave the door wide open while she turns her back to me and waits for me to fill the cup. I feel such humiliation at this point. I cannot believe the events that have unfolded since I woke up. The entire ship is waiting for me to fill this cup so that the Captain can determine what to do with me once the results come back. Only once the drug tests are finished and the investigation is completed to their satisfaction will the Captain be given permission by the shoreside authorities to grant crew shore leave. Every crew member in the Crew Bar is holding their breath, waiting for my results.

The washrooms are down a corridor not far from the Crew Bar. All three groups of crew members are standing around the large, open space patiently waiting for me to fill this cup. With the women's washroom door and the bathroom stall wide open, every sound I make can be heard by everyone. Everyone waits in silence and listens to me fill this plastic container. It is a tense moment as I pull my shorts and underwear down and fill the cup. My stream of urine fills only half of the plastic container. My stomach is still full of water but with no breakfast. I wipe myself, put the orange lid back on the plastic cup, and walk toward the sink to wash my hands. I wrap the container in paper towel and hand it over to the officer.

"That's all I have in my bladder," I tell her. The female officer walks me out of the washroom and back to the holding area in the Crew Bar. I walk pass the two hundred male crew members who have just heard me urinate and I glance at my boyfriend. I keep walking toward my supervisor who points to a chair for me to sit in across from the officers.

My plastic cup of urine is taken to another area for testing and SECO is waiting patiently with radio in hand. The Captain is waiting on the other end of that radio on the Bridge with all the other Bridge Officers. The entire crew is anxiously waiting for the Captain's announcement to grant crew shore leave. The time is already approaching 11:00 a.m., almost three hours since the ship has docked. The entire ship is waiting for my results. The crew members standing in the Crew Bar with me were summoned at 8:00 a.m. when the authorities came onboard.

My supervisor had been searching for me since 8:00 a.m. when I was still sleeping in my boyfriend's cabin. I left his cabin around 8:15 a.m. and was in the Crew Mess by 9:00 a.m. My boyfriend had been summoned to the Crew Bar for the drug test shortly after I left his cabin. When the search warrant was set out for me, he knew I was probably in the Crew Mess eating breakfast, yet he did not say where I was because he really was not sure. I could have already finished breakfast and been in the chapel practicing piano, or at the gym working out, or on the crew deck sunbathing, or in the Crew Library on the computer. He really didn't know where I was. All he knew was that I would go ashore at some point and return to the ship in time for his break so we could have some time together before I started my shift at 7:00 p.m. My supervisor knows I have a boyfriend, but she has no idea know who he is, she does not know where his cabin is located, and she certainly doesn't know what I do in my time off. I definitely am not about to divulge any of that information to her.

SECO holds the radio tight in his hand as he paces back and forth waiting for my urine results. As the Chief Security Officer of the Security Department, SECO never has had to deal with a drug mule on any of his ships, and it's clear he doesn't know how he is going to deal with a possible suspect who is a woman and a North American from the Entertainment Department. He looks at me and his eyes speak volumes as our eyes lock. He knows I am innocent; he knows I am clean. I know he knows that I am clean. How will he carry out the investigation if the results came back that I am clean? If the urine test comes back and determines I am guilty, I will be immediately handcuffed and taken off the ship.

The shoreside authorities insist that drugs were brought onboard from Jamaica to be delivered to St. Thomas, and the police are waiting for answers. The dogs have sniffed all the cabins and did not find anything. The dogs were in my cabin while I was in my boyfriend's cabin. Nothing was found there, and when the dogs sniffed me, nothing was found. Finally, the urine test comes back and the results are negative. A sigh of relief comes over my supervisor's face. The shoreside police give SECO the results. Immediately, SECO radios the Captain on the Bridge. He tells him clearly so all the Bridge Officers can hear, "She is clean. Investigation completed here with these two hundred crew members."

Now the police and their dogs are to stand at the gangway for the next part of the search. The dogs will sniff each passing crew member as they leave the gangway. As soon as SECO radioed the Captain, a sigh of relief swept through the entire Crew Bar. SECO motions all crew members to leave, saying, "Thank you for your cooperation."

I stand up to leave but my supervisor approaches and blocks me. "Lincee, I know you are not required to carry your pager when off duty, but can you please carry it in case of emergencies? We never know when the authorities will come onboard for a random drug test." I look at her and reply, "Yeah, I will carry it, and by the way, don't EVER embarrass me like that again. I did not appreciate you telling everyone here that my bed was not slept in last night."

I do not wait for her reply and walk past her to head down to my boyfriend's cabin on Deck Three. The Captain finally makes the announcement, "Attention! Attention! Crew shore leave is now granted. I repeat, crew shore leave is now granted."

I reach below deck in Zone Three and I knock on Anthony's door. He opens it and I step inside. He opens his arms and immediately I fall into his embrace. He apologizes, "Lincee, I am so sorry you had to go through such an ordeal. It was so embarrassing for you. Sorry."

I sigh deeply into his arms. "I am so pissed at my supervisor with her questions. I am so hungry too. I didn't even get to eat breakfast."

"I know why you were supposedly randomly called for the drug test. It's because I am Black. It's your association with me that alerted security," he explains.

I already knew since I joined the ship last week that my reputation had spread throughout it like wildfire; within twenty-four hours I already befriended a sailor which meant that I was not available for anyone else. My heart softens as he hugs me. My ordeal is over, but now my reputation will continue to spread like another wildfire after this incident.

Chapter 8
Down Under

It is not that life at shore is distasteful for me. But life at sea is better. Sir Francis Drake

The ship has left the port of Sydney, Australia after embarking 2,600 new passengers and a new set of crew members to replace the leaving crew. All the provisions have been restocked and the galleys are preparing the meals for the first night of sailing for these new passengers. It is a beautiful, smooth sailing as we head south along the coast toward Hobart, Tasmania. We have a full day at sea tomorrow and then we are to arrive in the port of Hobart the day after early in the morning. I am excited to go ashore because I plan to visit the Bonorong Wildlife Sanctuary.

I am thrilled to explore Australia and New Zealand. I never dreamed I would have the opportunity to do so. After passing my probationary short-term contracts, which each only lasted a few months, I am eager to start my first permanent contract and am ecstatic to be assigned to this ship for a period of six months. Actually, I am beyond excited to have taken a sabbatical from my life on land. I sincerely thought I would never in a million years be working at sea full-time as it certainly does not cover my monthly expenses back home. Working at sea has created a deficit in my pocketbook, but I am content knowing that this is just a six-month stint and I will resume my life and salary back home once I finish this contract. Money cannot buy this experience. I must live it; fully experience the excitement and adventure that lays ahead. Moreover, I am delighted I have my boyfriend, Anthony, with me again for this contract to enjoy making memories with and exploring the various ports of call.

I finish my evening shift and quickly head to my cabin right afterwards to freshen up for the Sunday night crew church service. Instead of going to the Crew Bar with my colleagues to unwind after work, I prefer to attend the quiet church service for my weekly mental and spiritual charge. I pack my large bottle of water, a few white barf bags in case I come across some contraband to transport, and my Bible in my bag. I walk to the Staff Mess along the i95 and open the heavy steel doors leading into the mess. Once again, I am the only female crew member in attendance greeting all the male crew members before we start the service. I continue to actively participate in the Christian church services for the crew. I take turns with another crew member in delivering sermons and leading Bible studies on Wednesday evenings.

I have such a fruitful day and evening that I manage to fall quickly into a deep sleep this Sunday evening. The next morning, when I arrive at my station in the Entertainment Department to start my shift, my supervisor asks me to come into her office to talk. I don't think anything of it and so I walk in and ask, "What's up?"

She looks straight into my eyes and tells me, "Lincee, I had a meeting last night with the Cruise Director and he informed me there is no one onboard quite qualified to lead the weekly passenger Sunday morning church services. Since we are sailing from Australia to New Zealand for the next four months, the Entertainment Department needs to provide a Sunday morning service to the passengers who are requesting one. Head Office will not be sending a minister to lead the Sunday services and the passengers do not want a Catholic service. They are requesting a Protestant service." She pauses, takes a breath, and continues. "I know you are a part of the Christian Seafarers' church service and have provided services for the crew. Would you consider assisting the Cruise Director to deliver sermons to the passengers every Sunday?"

We look at each other for a few moments of silence. I am in utter shock, to put it mildly. I never expected this to come from my supervisor nor did I ever expect in a million years to be ministering to passengers at sea. This is an opportunity and a surprise to say the least. I feel deeply humbled that my Christian reputation has reached the desk of the Cruise Director and he is requesting my service to fulfill the passengers' needs on Sundays in a specific lounge. After the shock subsides, I finally answer my supervisor. "I would be glad to be of any assistance to the Cruise Director, just let me know what to do."

"Go to the Cruise Director's office now; the CD is waiting for you!" She dismisses me from my morning duties, and I am on my way. As I head to his office, I am still in an utter state of disbelief. It takes about ten minutes to get from my supervisor's office to the CD's office as this is a much larger ship that carries 2,600 new passengers every twelve days and 1,200 working crew members. I silently pray for wisdom and the right words to speak as I walk to the Cruise Director's office with much nervousness in my heart and my mind racing with thoughts.

"Thank you God, for this opportunity. I know I am not a qualified minister, and I feel ill-equipped to deliver sermons to 2,600 passengers every Sunday. Please guide me and give me wisdom." My hand finally reaches the door handle of the CD's office in Zone One Deck Five. I open the heavy steel camouflaged door and enter inside.

"Lincee, you are here! Thank you so much for coming this morning. I just got off the telephone with your supervisor. Please come inside my office so we can talk," the CD cheerfully welcomes me.

"Hello sir, it's a pleasure to see you," I reply.

"The Assistant Cruise Director and I are so relieved that you are willing to assist us. We would like to welcome you to entertain on Sundays in a specific lounge. We will arrange for your schedule to be modified so you do not have additional hours of work and duties. Every Sunday morning you will start your shift and join the passengers in the main lounge to lead a religious service. How do you feel about this proposed idea?"

"Sounds like a great idea! However, I have a few requests in order for a proper service to be conducted, such as a microphone, lights, musicians, and a set up crew." I reply politely to the CD.

"Whatever you need, you have!" he cheerfully replies in his American accent. We exchange pleasantries and introduce ourselves, sharing our backgrounds. He is delighted to learn that I have partaken in the Christian church services for the crew on several of my past contracts. Somehow I convince the CD to entrust me with all the details of the weekly Sunday morning services.

I leave his office knowing that now I must write at least two different sermons and prepare the entire church service for each twelve-day cruise for the next four months while we sail under this itinerary. That is two different Sunday services for the same passengers every twelve days. I also have different sermons to prepare for the crew every week because I have the same crew with me onboard for six months, but every twelve days I will have new passengers. Suddenly, I realize I need to do a lot of praying and ensure that I walk uprightly even more as now I have a new role in my job description. I have a feeling that the crew will start looking at me differently with my newly assigned tasks.

My duties suddenly include having the right church songs to match the message of the sermon. I need to find the right musicians willing to assist and serve in the Sunday morning services. I do not think it is appropriate if I conduct the entire service alone, delivering the prayer, playing the piano, and delivering the sermon. I manage to recruit two fellow musicians to assist despite it being hard to convince musicians to wake up early in the day. Musicians onboard generally perform late into the evenings and never work mornings, so for me to find and convince any musician onboard to wake up early to play church songs is a feat in and of itself.

There is a lot more work to do in preparing a weekly Sunday service for passengers than there is for the crew services. For the crew services, I am only in charge of delivering the sermon; I never once had to plan the whole service and the details of the communion. Now, for the passengers, I must start from scratch to prepare and program an entire service and recruit assistance. I really feel like calling some pastors back home on land as I feel in dire need of words of wisdom. With the time zone difference from Australia and the cost of a phone card, I know that making telephone calls of any long duration is not realistic. At this point, I am left to my own devices and wisdom, drawing from my past experiences of my church upbringing.

Each night after my shift, I now take the time to walk along the entire Deck Seven where all the main lounges and entertainment take place. I slowly walk through the different lounges to observe the conduct of the passengers. Whenever I held an event or hosted an activity in the past, I only paid attention to the adults in my scheduled activity. I never have had to pay much attention to the conduct and behaviour of passengers in other hosted activities. Now I have reason to do so and I watch everyone's behaviour. Normally I don't take time to observe my fellow colleagues. Now I want to watch how the entertaining crew members interact with the passengers because I want to see how the passengers behave throughout the week enjoying different types of entertainment on the different stages and lounges. I look at the passengers differently as I wonder who will actually attend a Sunday morning church service during their vacation holiday on a cruise ship. Onboard, we offer every type of entertainment from comedians and musicians to dancing and weekly interactive games. Watching how these passengers interact in the different lounges gives me an idea as to who may be attending my Sunday services. Are these people who drink endlessly be a disruptive type of audience full of hecklers? I scan the lounges to get an idea of who my passenger audience might be come Sunday morning.

Today is Saturday and the Cruise Director is finalizing the Sunday program of daily activities. He invites me into his office to look at the final draft of the Sunday cruise program before it goes to the printers. I see my name listed for the Sunday service at 9:00 a.m. My event is the first form of entertainment listed on the daily program. Most passengers will be sleeping in after attending the late show or gambling in the casino. Also, many passengers will be in the dining rooms or buffet enjoying their breakfast. I really do not anticipate a large turnout in the lounge I am assigned to deliver the service.

That night I walk by one lounge one last time before going to my cabin to turn in. The comedian is on stage and there are about twenty people scattered throughout a room that can hold about 600 people. I stay for a few minutes listening to the comedian and his crass humour leaves a sour taste. I am glad I am not a paying passenger who has this kind of entertainment option. I generally do not get to observe my fellow crew members during their shifts when they are entertaining passengers since I am working too. Plus, as soon as we crew finish our shifts, we disappear below decks to get away from the passengers. One hardly sees other crew members hanging around on passenger decks after their duties. Tonight, I make a point again to stay above deck in the passenger quarters to observe them as well as the entertainment crew members at their stations.

The next morning, I wake up extra early to start my Sunday. I stay in bed just a few minutes longer than usual to silently pray as my roommate snores in the bunk below me. This morning, I am a mixed bag of emotions, feeling excited, eager, nervous, and scared. As the cabin sways with each swell of the Tasman Sea, I think the rough seas will keep the passengers from attending this morning's service. I come down the ladder of my bunk bed and am ready to start my day. This is my first Sunday service and sermon I am to deliver to the passengers. I put on my formal blue uniform, skirt, blouse, and jacket. I brush my long, black, silky hair and put on my hair band to keep it from falling into my face. I head to the mess to have my breakfast before the day's events begin. The crew there are surprised to see me in my formal uniform as I sit down to eat. The rest of my team are already at work in their stations. I am the only one working in a different station this morning and so my colleagues do not see me dressed up in my formals. I finish breakfast and rush back to my cabin to brush my teeth. I grab my bag into which I stuff my large water bottle, Bible, and sermon notes to tow under my arm.

I arrive at the lounge thirty minutes early to ensure everything is in place and ready to go. My two musicians are already present; one is warming up on the piano and the other is adjusting the microphone and chairs. The sound man in the production booth is testing the lights and the microphone. I walk in and greet my fellow colleagues to go over the final details. Passengers start to trickle into the lounge at this point, and I am on stage sitting in the chairs set up for us. There are other crew members at the entrance of the lounge greeting and welcoming the passengers. We have no idea how many passengers will show up for this morning's service.

I see three men entering the lounge wearing black shirts with white collars. I grow nervous as I count these priests. A steady stream of passengers are coming into the lounge and it is only 8:50 a.m. The service starts in ten minutes. I now realize I have counted more than five certified ordained ministers and several priests sitting in attendance and I begin to feel quite anxious. A steady stream of passengers continues to flow into the lounge, and I start to think that every white man coming into the room is a minster of some sort or a pastor from Australia or New Zealand sailing on this itinerary. Suddenly, I feel ill-equipped to deliver the sermon. I silently pray before the clock strikes nine o'clock. "God help me, give me the words to speak to your people." I ready myself to deliver my sermon about patience (appendix 2).

Dan the drummer gets up from the seat beside me and walks towards the pulpit to greet the hundreds of seated passengers. Every seat is taken, and people are still coming in as Dan starts the service with a prayer. Silence fills the lounge as he prays and then Patsy starts to play "The Old Rugged Cross" on the piano. Everyone is standing, singing the hymn. People are still filing into the lounge and standing in every inch available. I am in shock to say the least. I cannot believe the lounge is a packed house. After the service is over, Patsy, Dan, and I stay in the lounge as the passengers come up to shake our hands and greet us. The priests and ministers in collars shake my hand and I feel such immense honour; I am humbled to hear their reassuring comments about how they enjoyed the service. Many passengers stay behind for another thirty minutes to greet one another, chat, and shake hands with us three after the service just a like real church service. I see the Deputy Cruise Director and the Cruise Director at the back of the lounge who have been there throughout the entire service observing. They are now greeting many of the passengers, some of whom are offering positive feedback.

The lounge clears out about thirty minutes after the service is over and now the crew must set up for the next form of entertainment to be held here. Dan, Patsy, and I meet with the Cruise Director for some feedback. He is flabbergasted to say the least.

"Oh, my goodness. You packed the house. It was standing room for over one hour! The passengers loved the service and gave such positive feedback," he cheerfully tells the three of us before continuing, "The passengers are eager for the next Sunday service. Well done, team!"

Patsy, Dan, and I smile and agree that we all have enjoyed the morning service and greeting the passengers. Generally, when crew are finished entertaining on stage, they get off stage quickly through the backstage and disappear. The passengers disperse without any communication with the entertaining crew members. This morning is different, and I thoroughly enjoyed every minute of it.

The Deputy Cruise Director then chimes in, "The comedian last night in this lounge only had a handful of passengers for his set, and you three packed the house. Absolutely unbelievable! All 600 seats were taken, and many were standing."

The three of us smile as we leave the Cruise Director's office. Dan and Patsy return to their cabins as their next shift does not start till 5:00 p.m., and I rush back to my cabin to wash my hands thoroughly as I have just shaken about three hundred passengers' hands. I change out of my formal uniform and into my other uniform that is comprised of shorts, short-sleeved shirt, and a pair of white sneakers. This attire is much more comfortable for entertaining. It was a successful Sunday service, and the sermon seemed to hit the hearts of the passengers. I take a moment to pray and thank God that the whole event was successful as I head out my cabin door to start my 11:00 a.m. shift. In my heart, I am already eager for next Sunday to arrive.

Chapter 9
Captain's Hearing

Life is either a daring adventure or nothing at all.
Helen Keller

Our ship is docked overnight in Venice for a total of two days. I am so excited to be back at sea for another full-time contract, especially in this part of the world. I am thrilled beyond words to have this time to explore the entire Mediterranean, visiting many countries on this itinerary, for the next six months. This contract offer was too lucrative to turn down and staying on land teaching clients in the gym pales in comparison.

I decided to extend my sabbatical from my life on land and explore this opportunity that has come across my path. After returning home from my last contract touring Australia and New Zealand, I found it very hard to adjust to life on land and leave my boyfriend at sea. I worked in the gym instructing clients for about three months before I felt the urge to sail again. My heart yearned to be at sea once more to experience the adventures that awaited me. I carefully considered my options—life on land or life at sea. I could feel the sailor's blood running through my veins. Despite a hard start, with a bad experience with that Croatian Officer, I already had a good taste of life at sea, exploring itineraries such as Alaska, the Caribbean, and down under.

So naturally, when the Mediterranean offer came along, the decision was quite easy, despite of it meaning another deficit in my pocketbook for another six months. I prayed about the opportunity and realized that money cannot buy some experiences and life must be lived. I consider this contract a once in a lifetime opportunity and I certainly do not want to live with any regrets. So today, I am eagerly anticipating my arrival in Venice to join the ship.

While I pack my luggage in preparation for this Mediterranean contract, my mind constantly thinks about the sinking of the *Titanic*. In the film, as I recall, the passengers and crew did not have identification on them when they were rescued. For this reason, I decide to make a photocopy of my passport and put a copy of my passport on my phone just in case of emergencies. For example, if the ship were to be in some sort of distress and perhaps sinking, all the crew passports would still be locked in the vault of the crew office. I pack a small, transparent, waterproof bag that I can hang around my neck in case I need to produce proper identification. I carefully fold the paper copy of my passport and place it in the waterproof bag with a few hundred American dollars wrapped inside.

For my peace of mind, I want to ensure I have a copy of my passport with me if I happen to have amnesia and cannot remember where I am from; in such a case I would hopefully be speaking English and not another language, be rescued, and sent back to North America. I absolutely do not like to think of possible disasters, but I think it is better to be prepared and prudent as life has taught me. Life is full of surprises and sometimes when terror or trauma comes along one's path, usually at the least expected moment, it is hard to think straight when one is in shock or in pain. Little did I know that in due time I would need this waterproof bag with its strong lanyard hanging around my neck.

I finally reach the top of the gangway with my carefully packed two pieces of luggage and check into my officer's cabin to drop it off, happy to start my first contract as a promoted officer in my department. As an officer, I no longer have to share a cabin. I have my own privacy and a much larger space. My living quarters are an upgrade from my previous cabin on the other ship; that was a ten by eight feet cabin below the water line on Deck Three. I have a window in this cabin which means I am above the water line. My cabin has a seating area with a coffee table, and the entire living quarters are about fifteen by ten feet. I also have a much larger bed that fits two and an extra bunk bed above if I want to house a guest should I invite a family member or friend to cruise with me. As an officer, I no longer have to share a washroom plus I have a mini fridge in my cabin. All these small luxuries at sea make for better living conditions.

Moreover, I have access to the officer's laundromat which means, hopefully, no one will steal my undergarments.

I am so eager for this chapter to unfold that I do not know where to begin as I stand in shock in my cabin staring at my surroundings. We are in Venice for another day before we must sail, so I have some time to rest and adjust to the time zone change and walk around the ship to meet some of the crew. After I familiarize myself with the ship, locating the laundry facilities, the Officer Mess, Crew Office, Cruise Director's office, Print Shop, Crew Bar, and Library, I go back to my cabin to unpack. Shortly after I start, I hear a knock at my door. My cabin steward introduces himself and we chat for a bit. After thirty minutes, I walk over to the Security Department to take my picture for my crew identification. I listen intently as the security crew members speak to one another in Hindi, and I automatically go to the allocated place for the pictures and prepare for the next step. The security team is surprised to see me follow the process without being told. Little do they know that I comprehend Hindi more than I let on or can speak. I smile and exchange a few pleasantries in Hindi with these security crew members. It is always good to have the security force on your side as one never knows when you may need a favour or some extra protection.

I try to settle into my new environment and the time zone change. I manage to fall quickly into a deep sleep my first night onboard. Suddenly, the telephone rings and wakes me up. I look at the clock and it reads 3:00 a.m. The telephone continues to ring, and I get out of bed and reach over to my desk to answer. I do not even answer the phone with a hello. I pick up the receiver and start with, "This better be good because it's 3:00 a.m." I am very annoyed.

"Hi, Cheryl! May I come over now?" a man speaks in drunken, slurred speech with a Filipino accent.

"You got the wrong number!" I retort back, slamming the phone down and crawling back into bed.

Within another minute, the phone rings again. I am getting pissed off at this point. I get out of bed again and pick up the receiver without saying a single word.

"Hello, Cheryl! I am coming over now," the same man speaks in the same drunken, slurred, Filipino accent.

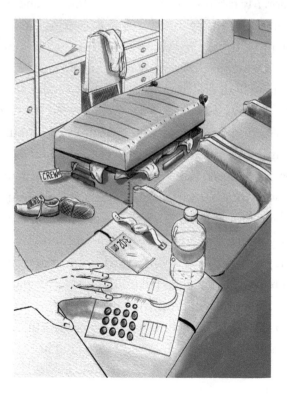

"There is no Cheryl here. She disembarked. I am the new officer in this cabin. Do not call here again!" I shout this back so he can hear me clearly in his drunken state because he clearly cannot hear that I spoke with a North American accent and sound nothing like the woman he is calling for.

Afterwards, I have a hard time falling back asleep. Knowing I must get up in less than three hours, I toss and turn for the rest of the night. I start my day tired and feel like my gas tank is only half full. I cannot wait for the day to end so I can sleep again. I look at my work schedule and it looks like I have a break in the afternoon so hopefully I can take a nap to help my adjustment to this time zone.

I enjoy my privilege of being able to eat in the Officer Mess, but very quickly I learn that the posted weekly menu and food is the same boring, bland menu with no spice or variety as the food in the Staff and Crew Messes has. Despite being an officer, today I decide to go to the Staff Mess and look for different options for lunch. As I walk inside, all the crew look up, surprised to see an officer in the Staff Mess walking along the buffet line with tray in tow. I am out of place amid the rank below me. Generally, officers do not eat in the mess of a rank below them nor are their cabins in the same quarters; they typically stay in the ship's officer quarters and eat in the Officer Mess. As an officer, I personally do not care about rank; the only privilege I really covet and appreciate is my single cabin and privacy. Food-wise, I go wherever it is delicious and the options are appealing. As I place the food on my plate and come to the end of the buffet line, I look around the tables to see where I can sit. I walk over to the security officers' table and ask if I may join them.

The security team welcomes me and immediately the group asks me as I sit down, "Why are you eating here in the Staff Mess? You are an Officer."

I smile back. "The food options here are better. Really, they are," I say as I bite into my forkful of spaghetti.

The security team members are shocked at my response as all crew know that officer food is the same quality as passenger food and the food in the Staff and Crew Messes are quite different to say the least. Over lunch, I enjoy befriending the security team personnel at this table as we chat between bites of our lunch. I take a liking to one of the security officers who also turns out to be one of the ship's firemen. His name is Amit. He has double duty—a police officer and fireman all in one. I see a twinkle in his eye as he speaks with me and I feel like I have just hit the jackpot. My plan now is to eat in the Staff Mess whenever I am able to going forward and sit at this table.

I am quite pleased to be sitting at this table of police officers and firemen. Much like the setting of a high school cafeteria, I see that all the tables around me are seated with people who have the same colour of uniform. The musicians sit at the same table with other musicians, the spa staff sits together, the boutique staff sit together, and the casino staff sit at the same table. Everybody sits with their own departments among their own colleagues. Nobody dares to sit with the security staff and firemen. I am not one bit afraid of the security personnel and they have welcomed me to their table when I bravely asked to join them.

After lunch, Amit escorts me back to my cabin. We enjoy the chat as we walk along the i95 corridor toward my cabin from the stern to the bow. I invite Amit inside my officer crew quarters and share with him my excitement at being a newly promoted officer. This is the first time I have an officer cabin and am excited that I have made my first friend onboard. I invite him to take a seat in the lounging area by the window. As the sun shines through the window, lighting up my cabin, I make a cup of tea for each of us to enjoy as we sit and talk. Amit is a very good listener and we exchange many stories. After some time, he leaves for his shift and I invite him to return this evening after our shifts to continue our fascinating conversation. I feel safe in his presence as he is a police officer and my only friend onboard this ship so far.

After my last shift of the day, I manage to grab a quick snack at the passenger buffet before heading back to my cabin to shower and unwind before Amit knocks on my door around midnight. I make us a hot cup of tea again as we sit by the window with our feet propped up, staring out looking at the moonlight glistening off the water. Our conversation and stories are so intriguing that we don't realize how quickly the time passes. The telephone rings, interrupting our conversation, and I look at the clock; it is 3:00 a.m. I ignore the phone, but it keeps ringing, so we stop chatting and I reach over to the desk to answer it. I hang up annoyed and Amit asks me, "Is everything alright, Lincee?"

"It's the same man who has called every night at 3:00 a.m. since I joined the ship. He's looking for someone named Cheryl and he keeps disturbing my sleep asking to come to my cabin," I reply in an annoyed tone.

Amit proposes a suggestion to me. "It's a good thing I am here in your cabin tonight to witness this harassment. Would you let me assist you in catching this perpetrator who is troubling you?" I am beyond relieved to accept this offer of assistance as I really am at my wit's end at this point. For the past four days, I have been dealing with the consistent harassment, lewd phone calls, and lustful stares gawking at me everywhere I move about on the ship. I really don't like being looked upon as fresh meat. I feel blessed to have this security officer in my cabin currently to witness the situation. We continue chatting while lounging by the window, and I share with him my ordeal of being harassed by the Filipino crew members since joining the ship. As I look out the window, I can see the moonlight reflecting off the water as the ship sails to Naples. I turn around and continue to tell Amit that all these sailors look upon me as prey and I absolutely loathe the lustful stares everywhere I go about on the ship. Amit is upset to learn of my situation and all the sexual harassment I have been dealing within such a short period. He can see it all makes me feel very uncomfortable.

As I further reveal my situation, Amit tells me he will set the wheels in motion to assist me in catching this sex predator out to get me. He will set up a situation to deter any other crew members from bothering me again for the remainder my contract. As our conversation unfolds, I see that he really cares for my safety and comfort, and he genuinely wants to help me. It is almost 4:00 a.m. by the time we finish talking and I am tired. Amit returns to his cabin and I manage to fall into a deep sleep. I am still adjusting to the time zone change. Thank goodness I can sleep in tomorrow when we dock in Naples as I do not start my shift till later in the afternoon. In the coming days, I learn that the security team onboard is a very powerful force to reckon with; every one of these security officers onboard are Navy trained and some are police officers back in their own countries who arc very well traincd and experienced in policing.

With each passing day, I wake up groggy and tired as my sleep is disturbed continually by the sexual predator and his harassing 3:00 a.m. phone calls. I learn that the women in my department are also now complaining about crank telephone calls in the middle of the night. After comparing notes, we realize it sounds like the same drunken crew member is calling all the women in the middle of the night after his drinking binge in the Crew Bar. At this point, I am livid learning of such harassment that has been an ongoing issue within my team and concerned that not one single person has reported the harassment. As an officer and leader of my department, I am eager to catch this perpetrator and have him reprimanded with the consequences. I immediately pick up the telephone and call SECO to make an appointment to discuss this serious matter. The Chief Security Officer immediately invites me to his office as he hears the urgency in my voice over the telephone.

I leave my station and walk into SECO's office at the opposite end of the ship which takes me about ten minutes to reach. Sitting in his office, I report the incidents and all the complaints from my department subordinates that are now submitted on paper as a testament. As I slide the papers across his desk, he is surprised to hear I have only been onboard the ship for six days and already I have been harassed to such a point. Immediately, he picks up the telephone and calls the COMMS Centre which is the central hub of communications on the ship. SECO requests that all the telephones in the following cabins be replaced with caller ID phones and that there is to be a tap on every one of these telephones belonging to the female crew members. The TAP report from the COMMS Centre will be sent to SECO each day plus he will review and search the closed-circuit cameras in the CCCTV room to identify who the perpetrator is and from where is he calling.

I leave the SECO's office relieved to know I have the police watching out for me and that an investigation is in motion. I return to my station about an hour later to inform the department of the update. The girls are relieved and we all head for lunch in the mess. While eating, my pager goes off and I see the number is from SECO's office. I return his call and he summons me to return to his office later this afternoon for a follow-up. I tell my security friend, Amit, over lunch about the events that have unfolded since he left my cabin last night. He offers to be of any assistance that I need.

After a long day, I return to my cabin to unwind and relax before heading to sleep. I am expecting Amit to stop by. I answer his knock on my door and welcome him inside as I set up a hot tea for us to enjoy. I turn off the lights and leave the nightlight on by my desk. We again sit on the lounging chairs by my window and stare out the window looking at the moonlight glistening on the waters as we sail throughout the night. Sitting side by side, we talk about our day and our conversation is a delight to my mind as he intellectually stimulates me and makes me laugh. We discuss many facets of life as the time slips away. Suddenly, the telephone rings and we realize time has slipped by so quickly that the clock now reads 3:00 a.m. Precisely the same time as the other nights, the same sex predator has called my cabin on cue. This time I have been instructed to keep him on the telephone to sweet talk him and illicit information. I have a list of questions to engage the caller and to get him to say my name several times during our conversation.

As I engage the caller, Amit looks at the caller ID window on my phone. He quietly slips out of my cabin and goes to the corridor where the call is coming from. The ID number on the telephone indicates the deck, zone, and exact location of the caller. While I continue to talk to the perpetrator, Amit swiftly and quietly walks down the corridor and stands a few feet behind the wall around the corner from the caller, listening in on that side of the conversation. Amit is out of sight of the ceiling camera as this caller is calling from a corridor located below deck in the crew quarters but in an intersection where a camera has been installed. Amit listens to the conversation and after a few moments hears the man say my name into the receiver. Amit jumps out and apprehends him.

The Filipino crew member in his drunken state tells Amit to back off and mind his own business. I can hear Amit through the telephone line. The crew member tells Amit that he is talking to his girlfriend and has done nothing wrong. Amit grabs the phone and says, "Lincee, is that you?" I reply back, "Yes, it's me on the other end. This is the guy who has been calling and harassing me!" Amit hangs up the telephone after telling me to stay inside my cabin for safety. The crew member fights Amit back and shouts, "You are not on duty as a police officer now, leave me alone!"

"I am undercover now, and you are caught!" Amit radios the Night Security Manager and immediately the scene is swarmed with the manager and police officers. They handcuff the drunken sailor and take him to the security quarters for further interrogation.

The next morning, I am paged before I even make it to work and am summoned to SECO's office at 9:00 a.m. I managed to only sleep from 4:00 a.m. to 7:30 a.m., and I am feeling tired as I start the day at sea with insufficient rest. As I head to SECO's office, I am eager to learn of the events that unfolded after I went to sleep last night. I open SECO's door and walk inside the office to see him, the Night Manager, and several other security officers. SECO tells me that the COMMS report indicates that the disturbing telephone calls have been coming from one location and the closed-circuit cameras depict the same crew member now displayed on the computer screen. SECO asks me to take a close look at the screen to see if I recognize this crew member.

"SECO, I just joined the ship six days ago. I do not know any Filipino crew members, nor do I associate with any Filipino crew members and I am not Filipino. I go to work and do not even go to the Crew Bar to socialize." I continue in dismay, "I don't know anyone on this ship and, even if I did recognize that man, I do not know who he is."

"We have investigated, and this man has been calling many women on this ship for quite some time, harassing the girls, and yet not one person has come forward to report the sexual harassment. Thank you for reporting this issue, Lincee. At the present time, the perpetrator is in the Captain's hearing with the officer who apprehended him last night. Rest assured, his sexual harassment toward you and all the female crew members will cease immediately. The Captain will summon you in a few moments and you are to report to Deck Twelve, portside. The security personnel here will escort you."

The Captain radios SECO and summons me to attend the hearing. I am immediately escorted up to the Captain's quarters and dropped off. Walking inside the room, I see Amit sitting in one of the chairs with the Staff Captain. I am warmly greeted and invited to sit down. The hearing continues once I sit down. Once the investigation and hearing are complete, the verdict is read as "guilty without fault." The perpetrator is sent to his cabin to pack his bags and will remain in isolation until he disembarks. He is dismissed from the company and will be sent home immediately when the ship docks the next morning and Head Office arranges for his flights home at his expense of being fired. I am shocked to hear the good news and results of the inquiry. I speak up. "Thank you for all your work in dealing with this situation, but it was not my intention to get the man fired. I just wanted his behaviour to stop."

The Staff Captain looks directly into my eyes, "Lincee, there is zero-tolerance for any type of sexual harassment of any kind on any vessel in this company. That crew member is dismissed because of his ongoing behaviour, and no one was brave enough to come forward and report it until now. Thanks to you, many of the women on this ship will now feel safer."

The Staff Captain then looks at Amit and back at me. At this exact moment, flashbacks of my encounters with the Croatian Officer come flooding to my mind. Why didn't I know how to report such crimes in the past? All those untold stories of crime, discrimination, and violence that I witnessed and experienced, and I never knew how to get justice until now. The Staff Captain interrupts my thoughts and continues, "I am glad to have this issue resolved, however, I do have one question that is puzzling me on how this sex predator was caught."

The Staff Captain turns to Amit and continues, "How is it that you, Amit, just happened to be in Lincee's cabin at 3:00 a.m. when that crew member called her cabin? You were not on duty at that time. What are you doing in her cabin at 3:00 a.m.?"

Amit looks at me and I remain stoic and silent as he looks back at the Staff Captain to answer his unexpected question.

I suddenly pipe up, "Isn't it enough that we have the issue resolved? We don't need to know how or what lengths were necessary to get the job done."

The Staff Captain looks at me and asks, "Yes, I agree, but I just don't understand how an officer who is off duty is able to be in your quarters to assist you at the precise time when the telephone rang."

Amit jumps in, "Sir, I was in her cabin last night after our duties. We are friends and we were talking."

The Staff Captain then turns to me, "I thought you said you don't have any friends onboard since you just joined the ship six days ago? Yet, you have the most reputable security officer in your cabin at 3:00 a.m.? How is this possible?"

Amit jumps in, "Sir, we are friends and I was in her cabin because I consider her to be my girlfriend."

"Alright here, case dismissed." The Staff Captain looks at me. "You have a very good friend here onboard," as he nods towards Amit and smiles.

Now the entire Officer Department and Captain know I have one friend on this entire ship, and he has just declared to them that I am his girlfriend. My reputation spreads within the short time I have been onboard this ship. I certainly did not expect to hear this piece of information, or revelation, to come from Amit at a Captain's hearing. I am just relieved that this whole ordeal is over, and I can rest easy for the remainder of my six-month contract.

I head back to my station to work, however, within twenty minutes, the telephone rings. I pick up the receiver thinking it is a passenger calling about the hours of operation. Instead, it is the same drunken Filipino crew member who has been harassing me for the last six days. He is sober and crying on the other end as he tells me he just got fired and is being sent home. He begs for my forgiveness and begs me to tell the Captain to save his job as he cannot go home to tell his wife he got fired for sexual harassment. I calmly reply back, "I forgive you. I did not fire you. You got yourself fired. Your constant inappropriate behaviour toward many of the female crew members got you fired. All I did was report the incident. It is better you go home so the female crew members do not have to deal with your inappropriate behaviour anymore."

"I beg you! I beg you! Please forgive me!" he pleads with me. At this point, my heart feels for this man as this job is his bread and butter for his family back home. I understand that a sailor at sea is lonely and sexually frustrated, yet this is no excuse for his behaviour.

I answer back, "I said I've already forgiven you, but I will not go back to the Captain. Good-bye!" I hang up the telephone irritated, and my heart no longer feels sorry for this crew member. Even though he has been fired, he can easily apply for a job with another cruise line. I sit and think back to my past encounters with the Croatian Officer and shake my head. Karma always catches up! Even though I cannot see that Croatian Officer get his karma, I know that one day it will bite him back for what he did to me. And today this Filipino sailor got what he deserved; his long-awaited Karma has just bit him back.

Chapter 10
Terror at Sea

I'm not afraid of storms, for I'm learning how to sail my ship.
Louisa May Alcott

*N*ews of this Filipino crew member being dismissed and sent home spreads like wildfire amongst the crew, which is comprised of approximately eighty percent Filipino out of the 1,200 crew members. With each passing day, hatred towards me grows amongst the Filipino crew members, a group that predominantly makes up every department. They believe I sent their paisano home. News about me being protected by the security team also spreads and not one single person dares to make my life difficult despite me often getting dirty, rude, and sneering looks as I move about the ship. I feel disgusted at the menacing, angry looks from the Filipino male crew members, but I have no fear as I always have a security team member moving about the ship with me. Also, being of officer rank and a North American who is not Filipino, no one dares to mess with me after they hear about what I did to protect the women onboard. There are only a few

Filipina females onboard the ship, and only one female Filipina officer in the accommodation department and she is on my side, glad I reported that sailor and he got sent home.

As our ship sails the Mediterranean and visits both sides of the entire boot of Italy through the Adriatic Sea and the Mediterranean, I begin to relax further with each passing day. Life is good as I slowly settle into the routine and excitement that awaits me each day as I wake up to a new port of call or new country. At this point, I cannot imagine going back to my life on land. Once the sea touches your heart and soul, life on land never is the same.

Today as I go ashore in the Italian city of Civitavecchia, I notice the security team at the gangway is a bit tense and the camaraderie between the crew members is strained. I spend quite a bit of time with each of these security personnel, so I notice when something is off. Moreover, I understand Hindi more than I let on so, when I am amongst those crew members, I spend more time listening than speaking. Often, other dialects seep into the conversations, such as Marathi, Telugu, Konkani, and Gujarati. I also thoroughly enjoy practicing my Bulgarian with the Slavic crew members and pick up a few new phrases each day. The Bulgarian officers love it when I speak Bulgarian with them as it really throws them off with my perfect pronunciation coupled with my North American English and Scottish accent. These officers are teaching me more than my own Bulgarian tutor back home. Immersing myself in daily conversations with such a diverse, multi-ethnic group of crew members satiates my mental appetite for learning. My primary focus in maintaining these languages is to ensure I have the accurate diction, enunciation, and comprehension while communicating

After my time ashore in Civitavecchia, I get ready for my evening shift with anticipation for the day to be over so Amit and I can get together to share about our days. I am eager to tell him all about my experience ashore and to inquire about the tension I noticed amongst the security department at the gangway.

There is a new Security Supervisor who has recently joined the team which is comprised of twelve police officers. He is quite arrogant, and every day he relentlessly makes life very difficult for every member of his team, to say the least. Today, after the ship left the harbour of Civitavecchia, karma unfolded for this man. Amit relates to me the entire story and all the escapades of the arrogant supervisor.

Amit tells me that, earlier in the day, one of the security personnel convinced this arrogant supervisor to meet him later that evening at the mooring station at the stern of the ship where the mooring ropes are kept and where no cameras are installed. He offered to hand over the contraband of alcohol and cigarettes to this supervisor where there is no recording evidence and conversations can't be heard over the loud sound of the propellers and the splash of the wake behind the ship. Thirty minutes prior to the pre-arranged time for the supervisor's arrival, the entire security team meets at the mooring station while SECO is working in the office with Amit. They draw all the blinds, go over the plan as discussed, and then proceed to hide throughout the mooring station waiting for this supervisor to show up. At the appointed time, the Security Supervisor arrives on Deck Five, Zone Five, making his way to the mooring station. Once he enters the area, he turns and carefully locks the heavy steel door behind him to ensure privacy. He walks towards the security member who is standing at the very end of the ship which has a railing overlooking the wake of the ship. There is a heavy steel grate along the railing so that nothing can fall over the back of the ship.

The supervisor starts to speak in Hindi to ensure no one else can understand as he barks orders to be given the contraband. He is facing the crew member whose back is against this railing. Slowly, the entire team of security personnel, ten in total, crawl out of hiding and tiptoe towards this unsuspecting supervisor. As his back is towards the door rendering him unable to see the entire security team, they are able to quickly grab hold of him before he becomes aware of their presence. One security officer switches off all the lights. The lone security member who convinced the supervisor to come carefully unlatches the metal grate attached to the railing. All ten security personnel push the supervisor to the railing, flip him upside down, and hang him over the railing by his ankles. Four security men are now holding onto his ankles with two pairs of hands on each ankle. One security crew member is holding him by his belt to ensure the other four pairs of hands do not slip while holding onto his ankles.

SECO is working in the Security Office writing up the day's report at the bow of the ship while Amit keeps him occupied. Amit knows what is happening at this precise moment and his conscience has told him not to be involved at the mooring station with the rest of his team. Meanwhile, during his chat with SECO, the Security Supervisor is hanging by his ankles at the stern of the ship screaming for his life. Shouts of Hindi and begging come from the mouth of this arrogant man promising to never threaten or make life difficult again for any of his team members. The cold Mediterranean waters splash up approximately a hundred feet spraying him with seawater. It is a crisp, cold, dark night as he hangs upside down looking at the moonlight bounce off the water beneath him.

One slip of these crew members' hands would send this arrogant supervisor headfirst to his death. The suction of the ship's wake would pull him into the propellers in no time which would chop him into pieces for the wildlife at sea to snack on. No evidence would be found of this missing crew member, and no cameras are present to record the movement at the back of the ship. The panicked howls of this crew member cannot be heard against the splashing of the loud wake chopping up the water. No one would suspect any foul play or find any evidence of a crime as this security team comprises the very people who investigate crimes and maintain order onboard for the passengers and crew. No fingerprints or footprints would be left behind, no fingers pointed, and no more threats from this arrogant supervisor to suffer under. Only the heart of conviction would remain to pierce and haunt the souls of these sailors for their organized crime to be rid of another human being!

After much begging and promises from the screaming supervisor, the security team pulls him back up over the ship's side railing. They close the grate and lock it against the railing once more. The supervisor is now standing soaking wet, covered with the saltwater, and surrounded by the fellow crew members in his team who all stand with their arms crossed against their chests. Back home, these strong men are military men and police officers in their own respective ranks in their precincts. This retired Navy supervisor knows better than to utter another word as he looks at the menacing faces of the crew circled around him. He is in for a small beating before they leave him on the ground of the mooring station. This Security Supervisor knows he is in for a rough contract if he stays another day on this ship. The entire security team is against him, and SECO and Amit are nowhere to be seen during this entire incident. SECO has retired to his cabin and left Amit in the office to finish up the paperwork.

Amit continues to further tell me the story of how the supervisor goes back to his cabin shaking in his boots after this entire ordeal. He is stuck because it would be his word against the entire team. He knows better than to cause any more problems because these fellow police officers can call back home to India and arrange to have gangs attack his family and make life even more difficult for him. The supervisor must devise a plan to end his contract immediately and not have to face his team members when the sun rises the next day. He finds a telephone in a quiet corner along the crew corridor and calls back home to check on his family, making sure they are okay and speaking in Hindi so nothing can be deciphered or traced back to his cabin.

Amit continues to confidentially reveal to me that immediately after the supervisor hangs up the telephone, he pages SECO to inform him that he must disembark the ship in the morning and head home due to a family emergency. SECO calls the Crew Office to immediately contact Head Office to arrange flights as soon as we dock the ship. SECO believes this made-up story of a family emergency while the supervisor packs his bags in his cabin. Within two hours, Head Office books the flights and emails the ship the flight itinerary. SECO is informed and the documents are prepared for the arrogant supervisor to disembark the moment the gangway touches ground in less than ten hours.

In the morning when the ship docks, with disembarkation papers in hand and luggage in tow, the supervisor walks across the gangway, head down so as not to make any eye contact with the security crew members of his team. He is escorted by an officer from the Crew Office who now hands over his passport and flight papers. The port agent greets him at the bottom of the gangway and takes him away in the prearranged vehicle to transport him to the airport. The ordeal is now over for the entire security team and a sigh of relief comes over all the team members. Hopefully, the Security Supervisor has learned his lesson to never be a bad leader and to never make life difficult for those who work for you and with you. It is a heavy lesson learned.

What a story Amit has shared with me and it leaves me just shaking my head in utter disbelief. Amit reminds me that what happens on a ship does not always stay on a ship; it can trickle back home when one messes with the wrong people. The security force onboard this ship, or any ship, is one not to be reckoned with as many of the crew know that these are military men back home. Several of the members also come from corrupt police forces in their homeland and can make life very difficult for family back home if you step out of line onboard, thousands of miles from your home and loved ones. Not one crew member steps out of line in the face of the security personnel on this ship. I am delighted to have each of them as my personal guard when I roam about the ship as we sail throughout the Mediterranean for the remainder of my contract.

Today our ship arrives in Venice for turnaround day to disembark passengers and offload the crew members who have finished their contracts. Our ship is docked overnight in Venice for a total of two days to restock and welcome passengers and joining crew members. It is a beautiful autumn day with overcast clouds and a hint of breeze. After a day ashore with a few team members exploring the Piazza San Marco, strolling through the cobbled streets with gelato in hand, I return to the ship to prepare for my evening shift. I look out the window as I get into my uniform and notice the wind has picked up and gondolas along the canal are knocking against each other with the swells of the water. The creaking sounds of the ship are growing more frequent and louder despite the mooring ropes tied down tightly around the bollards along the pier.

As I head out of my cabin and towards my workstation, I feel the ship slightly move and the creaking sounds of metal scraping intensify. I do not think much of the movement or noises as we are docked in Venice for another twelve hours. The wind has picked up and the ship starts to move which it should not be because the mooring ropes are tied to each of the bollards along the pier at the bow and stern. As I get out of the crew elevator on Deck Twelve and head toward my workstation, I feel a sudden, hard shift of the ship and a shuddering throughout the entire back of it in Zone Five. Beneath my feet, I feel as if I am standing on a trembling earthquake as the entire ship is now shaking intensely like a huge seismic event. Suddenly, the entire ship goes pitch black as the lights go out, including the emergency lights. Screams from the passengers ripple throughout my entire zone on every deck. The crew alert signal immediately is triggered and bells ring in the darkness. As a crew member trained in emergency situations, I never expected this precarious situation to unfold while docked in port. The vagaries of the weather at sea are full of surprises. Sudden changes can surreptitiously creep up on an unsuspecting sailor.

The back of the ship is now swinging away from the pier as the 300-ton, steel port bollard rips off the asphalt and swings deep into the aft of the ship on Deck Four. The flying bollard pierces the metal slats of the mooring station, creating a giant hole and leaving mooring ropes whipping in the wind and slashing against the water. The Bridge Officers immediately turn on the thrusters on the port side in hope of aligning the ship back along the pier but with no success.

A ship's ballast is used to provide stability to the vessel at sea. The ballast weighs the ship down and lowers its centre of gravity. These ballast tanks are connected to pumps that pump water in and out. Insufficiently ballasted boats tend to tip or heel excessively in high winds. Too much heel may result in the ship capsizing. If a sailing vessel needs to voyage without cargo, then ballast of little or no value is loaded onboard to keep the vessel upright. Some or all of this ballast is then discarded when it's replaced by cargo. With this heavy wind and hole in the back of the ship, there is no longer stability on this luxury cruise ship even with the ballast pumping water. The precious cargo on this vessel is us crew and passengers which are now at risk of danger.

The strength of the wind is now pushing the entire ship portside away from the pier and we hear the metal creaking of the steel hull pull on the forward bollard, slowly tugging it off the asphalt of the pier. Darkness continues to pervade the ship, and the screams of the passengers intensify as the crew try to calmly navigate to the crew exits. Once I enter through the crew exit door into the crew corridor, I see the emergency lights along the floor are lit up just enough for the crew to return to their cabins and gather their life jackets before heading to their emergency muster stations for duties.

The forward steel bollard has now also broken off the pier and punctured a giant hole in the front hull of the ship. The Bridge Officers are trying to take control and steer the ship, but with two heavy 300-ton bollards on either end of the ship pulling it into the water there is no way to release the mooring ropes. The entire ship is slowly being pulled down into the water starboard side first. The ship is doomed to sink within due time. The entire ship is listing starboard, and everything and everyone is leaning as the crew quickly and calmly rush to get lifejackets from their cabins below deck. As I manage to get down to Deck Four from Deck Twelve through the mad rush of crew members along the staircases, I constantly scan the crowds looking for Amit.

I finally am inside my cabin and can feel the ship severely listing as it further sinks. I pick up the phone and page Amit. My phone rings within a few seconds and it is him. I am scared and I urgently ask him, "Is it bad? Where are you? Which lifeboat will you be in?"

Amit speaks quickly and urgently to me. "No lifeboats, Lincee. The entire starboard side is sinking into the ocean. The wind has pushed the ship far from pier and both the steel bollards are pulling the entire ship down. No lifeboats will be dropped. Lincee, I love you! Go to Deck Seven and save yourself. I will find you. I love you. Go!"

"Amit, don't leave me. I don't want to die alone. I want to go with you. Where are you?" I cry back into the phone.

"Go Lincee, save yourself. I have duties; I will find you. Don't worry. If we die, we will go together! I love you!" Amit surprisingly declares his feelings for me again. If I perish today, at least I know I have one man who loves me.

The steel creaking sounds are getting louder as the listing of the ship intensifies. Everything slides off my desk as the ship lists to the right. I quickly grab my jacket to keep warm. Swiftly, I open my desk drawer and pull out my waterproof case that has a photocopy of my passport and a few hundred U.S. dollars tucked inside. I put the lanyard around my neck and tuck the plastic case inside my jacket as I quickly put my lifejacket over it all. I grab my hat and my pager and rush out of my cabin. All the crew members scurry along the crew corridors, rushing to the muster stations as required despite the frantic passengers who appear to be in a mad panic. No passengers are listening or staying in their muster stations since no lifeboats are being lowered. Passengers are also not listening to the Captain's announcements. At this point, the crew abandon their muster stations and head to the open deck. The entire starboard side is listing so much that it is impossible to walk straight.

Should the passengers and crew hit the water and be forced to swim, it will be each to their own. Regardless of what uniform one is wearing, upon finding ourselves in the cold waters, it will be each person fighting for their own life. No crew member in their right mind would try to help a passenger when everyone is swimming for their life. On the ship, when in uniform, crew members are trained to always assist passengers, especially in emergencies. If the ship hits the water, there is no rank amongst mankind; there is no passenger and crew status. The uniform no longer exists in the mind of a sailor as we are each fighting for our own lives.

I panic while trying to get to portside as the starboard side continues to sink quickly into the chilly water. Amit told me to go to Deck Seven portside; I hope to find him there as I scramble through the throngs of terrified passengers and push aside falling deck chairs. The Captain comes on making more announcements, trying to calm everyone as the lights throughout the ship flicker as the starboard side of the ship slips deck by deck beneath the water. The two heavy steel bollards on both ends of the ship are pulling the entire ship beneath the water as the ropes are wound tightly around them. All the elevator doors are open, but no elevators are present, revealing the empty shafts and interior steel ropes. Broken glass is strewn everywhere and screaming passengers are running rampant on every deck. Images of the sinking *Titanic* flash through my mind as I race along Deck Seven in search of Amit.

I finally make it to Deck Seven portside, running past fear-crazed passengers. The entire ship audibly creaks and sounds of grating metal screech louder and louder. Amongst the screaming crowds with my life jacket tightly wrapped against my chest, I frantically search for any security personnel and continue to look for Amit. My heart pounds with adrenaline, and in my mind I am preparing for the worst to unfold.

The crew of the entire Deck Department is split between the mooring stations at the bow and stern, desperately trying to release the mooring ropes from the ship so the 300-ton steel bollards can sink beneath the ship without pulling the vessel below water. The ropes are finally cut from the stern and that bollard sinks below, pulling and whipping the ropes out from the ship's mooring station. The entire stern of the ship now bounces up and down like a yo-yo beneath the water line as the ropes disappear from the ship and sink beneath the water. In a matter of minutes, the entire stern of the ship floats up above the water line, but now the bow of the ship is sinking as the forward steel bollard pulls those mooring ropes beneath the water.

All the passengers fall forward, and people are trampling over one another with screams of terror as the ship's stern and propellers are now above the water line. It is the scene of the sinking *Titanic* unfolding before my very eyes as the bow of the ship slips into the Mediterranean waters. I now run to the stern of the ship along Deck Seven on the portside with all the crew members and passengers beside me. I frantically look for Amit in the chaotic crowds. The passengers are still screaming and fighting to get to the back of the ship as the front of the ship is sinking into the water deck by deck, slowly being pulled down by the 300-ton bollard.

Every crew member is silent as they fight their way alongside the screaming passengers. We are trained to be calm and we are quiet as each of us fight for our very lives, grabbing onto anything that will pull us toward the stern. The entire bow of the ship is dipping beneath the water line as the Bridge Officers watch in horror while the ship sinks right before their eyes, diving headfirst into the waters. Deck chairs fly through the air along with people who don't have a good grasp on anything nailed down to the open deck. In the space of a few moments, I envision myself like the character Rose from the *Titanic* movie laying across the railing on the stern of the ship watching it sink in the cold waters. "Where is Amit?" I think to myself as I rush ahead of the terrified passengers and flying deck chairs. I am still frantically searching for him as I claw my way to the stern of the ship that is slowly rising into the sky. I know I must get to the back railing of the ship and lay on the other side just like the character Rose.

The heavy steel bollard remains tied to the mooring ropes and the sailors in the Deck Department are desperately trying to release the knot and unleash the ropes inside the mooring station at the bow. Every second is critically urgent as the water is pouring into the station and flooding around the crew members. The cold water is steadily rising up to their knees quickly. As the anchor is released and the mooring ropes are finally cut, the bollard pulls the ends of the ropes right out of the ship's hull. The entire bow of the ship starts to emerge out of the water and slowly surface again. Heavy steel cracking and bending sounds bellow above the screams of the passengers. The stern of the ship slowly comes down with the propellers dipping back into the water. Metallic creaking sounds still ripple throughout the ship against the screaming passengers and water pours all over the carpets as the ship starts to balance itself upright.

The passengers trample over the scattered, broken glass strewn across every deck as they run in all directions. As this crisis deepens, the deck chairs flying everywhere hit passengers and crew, which only exacerbates the already panic-stricken souls. The buoyancy of the ship further levels and soon the propellers are fully back beneath the water line and the bow of the ship is parallel to the entire ship above the water line. Screams and chaos still reverberate throughout the entire ship as lights continue to flicker. The images of the *Titanic* keep flashing before my mind as the unnerving events unfold.

The cruise ship now has two giant holes on the starboard side from the flying steel bollards, one in the bow and one in the stern. Some of the lights have come back on but no other electricity is running nor is the engine. The elevator doors on every deck remain wide open without any elevators. The Bridge Officers receive radioed shore-side assistance. No mooring ropes or anchor exist on the ship anymore, and the heavy winds continue to push the ship out into the dark, cold sea. I make it back to my cabin and my pager is beeping. I pick up the phone to call the beeping number with my lifejacket still on. It is my supervisor who tells me to go back to my station to ensure there are no fatalities there and to lock up for the night. I hang up, pissed off that I now I am required to walk up the flights of stairs from Deck Four to Deck Twelve from Zone One to Zone Five in this chaos of screaming, panicked passengers and broken glass everywhere.

I immediately page Amit. I wait anxiously for my phone to ring as I pace in my tiny cabin. After a few minutes, he calls me back. He assures me that he is okay, and I assure him I am well too. We agree to meet as soon as possible in my cabin after I complete my required duty at my station. I hang up the phone and navigate through the crew corridors and staircases to avoid the chaotic passenger areas. In the crew quarters, no one is screaming or freaking out, there is no broken glass at all, and the floors and staircases are clear to move about swiftly. Every crew member moves about quickly and quietly throughout the crew quarters to navigate to where they are needed, unhampered by pandemonium and screams and any hint of imminent danger. Within ten minutes, I make it to assigned location and quickly exit the crew door to check and lock up my station. I quickly rush back to the crew door to avoid any passengers and make it back to my cabin all within twenty minutes.

I enter my cabin and close the door behind me. As I start to take off my lifejacket, I hear a knock on my door. I swing open my door to see Amit standing before me. He rushes inside with relief and we embrace each other for a long time in our lifejackets. "I love you Amit! I am ready to die with you," I tell him.

"Me too, Lincee. I love you and am ready to die with you too," he replies in a soothing voice that just melts my heart.

The next day, after a full day at sea of entertaining passengers, I am quite tired as I head back to my cabin. I take a hot shower, get in my pajamas, and curl up under my blankets. I don't even turn on the television to listen to the news as I drift off to sleep. Amit is working the night shift, so I will not see him till tomorrow. The slight swaying of the ship rocks me quickly to sleep. I will not learn of the night's tragic events until later.

About 2:00 a.m., the Crew Bar starts to shut down. The DJ stops the music and the bar has served its last drink at 1:30 a.m. The crew start to leave, either to go back to their own cabins alone or with a newfound sex partner for the night, or to find a location without cameras to have a quick one with their newfound friend. Often the sailors have multiple sex partners, and frequently the women get their pick of the lot from whom is brave enough to seduce them on the dance floor. The crew generally get out of their uniforms and relax in their civvies in the Crew Bar as it is easier to lure a potential sex partner. It's often easier to get a woman's attention when she doesn't know what rank or what department you work in onboard. If you are wearing the uniform of a dishwasher or a laundry man, most likely you will not get a woman, or another sailor, interested in you. But if you walk in the Crew Bar wearing an officer's uniform, you'll most likely have every woman hanging off your arm all night.

Sailors know that to get the attention of the limited women onboard, they must remove their uniform, slap on some cologne, and be ready to show their dance moves and smile in desperate hope that a female sailor will even give them a glance. Some sailors do not even care which team you play for as long as you are willing to have sex, and when consent is mutual, then everything is for immediate pleasure. What generally happens on the ship, stays on the ship. Well, most of the time. Every night before heading to the bar, sailors raid the bowl of free condoms in the waiting room of the Medical Centre, and when those free condoms are all gone, they raid the condom vending machines. The condom machines are located right next to the phone card machines which are most often always empty as both are hot commodities at sea.

News about the night's events spreads quickly throughout the ship. I hear the crazy story the next day from multiple sources and Amit's security report confirms the true story. When the drunk sailors leave the Crew Bar, two Filipino crew members argue over one woman as to which cabin she should return to for a quick one. The arguing starts once the crew members reach the end of the corridor on Deck Eight. Since everyone rides down the elevator to each crew deck, crew members are getting off as the elevator stops on each floor. These two sailors and one Filipina girl head down to Deck Two, and the arguing continues with shoving as each sailor wants the girl to go to his cabin. The girl gets fed up and leaves quickly to head to her own cabin and sleep off the few drinks she had.

The two sailors become enraged, shouting back and forth in Tagalog, their native Filipino tongue. The loud arguing disturbs sleeping neighbours, yet no one dares to come out of their cabins to confront two drunken sailors arguing. The shoving escalates and one yells in Tagalog, "You have a wife back home, you don't need a girlfriend at sea. Let me have her!"

"I haven't seen my wife for five months of this contract and I won't see her for another five months until I return home!" the other sailor shouts back, again shoving his fellow crew mate.

"Back off! She was interested in me, and you tried to take her. Don't steal from me!" the first man shouts back in his slurred speech, waving his beer bottle in the air.

Suddenly, a rage of anger wells up in this man and he smashes the beer bottle on the handrail outside his cabin door. The top breaks off leaving a broken, jagged edge, and he lunges at the fellow crew member. He stabs the man's neck with the razor-sharp edge. Piercing screams fill the entire corridor as blood spurts forth in all directions. The sailor takes the beer bottle and stabs the man again and again. The piercing screams force other sailors out of their beds. They open their cabin doors to see a bloody fight between two sailors. Someone calls 911, and a few crew members jump in to peel the enraged sailor with the beer bottle off the other sailor. Blood is smeared all along the corridor walls, railings, floor, and cabin doors as the fight continues.

Amit is radioed by the Bridge and 911 team, and he radios for backup as he rushes down to Deck Two. The Bridge makes an announcement in the crew quarters below the passenger decks around 2:20 a.m., disturbing the sleep of everyone. The announcement pierces my cabin, waking me up from a dead sleep.

"Assessment Party! Assessment Party! Deck Two, Forward, Starboard side, Zone Two. "Stretcher Party! Stretcher Party! Deck Two, Forward, Starboard side, Zone Two."

Immediately after hearing this announcement, I know Amit will be called to attend to this incident. I am concerned for his safety as I know that this is the time the crew members are leaving the Crew Bar and most often are in an inebriated state and hungering for sex.

Amit arrives below deck to a gruesome scene with the fighting crew members covered in blood and one screaming in agony as blood spurts forth from his jugular vein. Shards of broken glass everywhere. Everyone is ordered to step back as the Night Manager, officers, security team, and assessment team along with the medical team step into the bloody scene. The stretcher party arrives ready to take the victim to the Medical Centre, but when they arrive to see such a bloody prospect, the amount of blood makes the team weak in the knees. With so much blood covering both crew members, they realize two stretchers will be required. Back up is called by the Senior Doctor. Additional security personnel are radioed to come and assist in stopping the fight between the two drunken sailors.

Fighting, screaming, pushing, shoving, and slipping on the bloody floor continues. Blood splashes everywhere, and the Night Manager and Amit are now covered with it while the security crew tries to separate the two sailors. Amit manages to get the broken beer bottle from the man wielding it so that he will stop stabbing, and the Doctor moves the slashed sailor onto the floor to apply pressure to his neck. Broken glass is rammed in his neck and the blood spurts forth splashing the Doctor's face. The two nurses are wide-eyed with fear; they look up at security for reassurance that they are safe to tend to the medical needs.

Eventually, the two sailors are placed on the stretchers and escorted by the security team members, who are also covered in blood, to the Medical Centre; the Senior Doctor runs alongside the stretchers too. The Assessment Party, comprised of four senior officers, radios for the Accommodation Department's crew supervisor to come clean up the bloody mess as soon as Amit completes the investigation and collects the necessary evidence. Amit quickly takes pictures of the scene for evidence and rushes to the Medical Centre for his own medical assessment. The Assistant Doctor looks over Amit to ensure he is okay from breaking up the fight before returning back to aid the injured sailors.

A few of the security personnel stay in the Medical Centre with the medical team while the drunken sailors are treated. Amit cannot even talk to the two drunken sailors to start his report because they are being medically treated, so he informs SECO that he will go back to the bloody scene and investigate the fellow crew members who witnessed the incident.

Amit finally leaves the crime scene to head into the security office to type up the entire security report. It is close to 5:00 a.m. when Amit is almost finished typing up the report. SECO returns to his office to find Amit with a distressed look on his face.

"Are you okay, Amit?" SECO asks with a concerned look on his face.

"I have never seen so much blood. I am in shock, sir," Amit admits without looking up from the computer screen.

"Yes, I know, Amit. I am in shock too. Please finish up the report and leave it on my desk. I will follow up later. For now, I need to get to the gangway as we dock in less than one hour. Do get some rest as your shift finishes in less than an hour," SECO tells Amit as he heads out the office door.

Amit sits back in his office chair, takes a deep breath, and looks at his hands that were recently covered with another man's blood. As he turns his hands over, he sees that he has washed thoroughly, leaving no traces of blood, but flashes of the scene just a few hours ago already haunt him as he looks at his hands. He picks up the pictures he took of the bloody scene and attaches them to the report for SECO to read prior to handing it over to the Captain. It is almost 6:00 a.m. when Amit leaves the office with the report in a file folder to come to my cabin.

I am sound asleep when he comes into my cabin. He puts the file folder on my desk and removes his uniform, then crawls into bed with me after washing his hands. He tries to sleep but is restless which wakes me up. "Hello, dear Amit. Good morning. How are you?" I ask as I nuzzle into his neck. He does not reply. He just holds me. After a few hours of amorous pleasures, I hop into the shower. Amit jumps in for a hot shower as I dress. I see the file folder on my desk, curious to look, but I wait till he comes out of the shower.

"What's that on my desk, Amit?" I ask.

"Lincee, something terrible happened last night. Did you hear the Bridge announcement last night calling for the Assessment Party?" he replies.

"Yes, dear. The announcement woke me up, but I fell back asleep shortly," I answer back.

"Lincee, I wrote up the report of the incident that unfolded last night and I have to give it to SECO before he gets back to the office at 9:00 a.m. I was in such shock while writing the report that I don't think I wrote it very well or very clearly. Would you mind looking at it and proofreading it before I submit it? This report will go to the Captain and Head Office within one hour of SECO reading, so it must be accurate and well written," Amit explains.

I have read several of Amit's reports in the past, so him asking me to proofread this report is nothing new. Amit continues, "But Lincee, I have to let you know, the pictures are very disturbing, and the report is gruesome. Will you be able to handle it? And keep it confidential?"

"Amit, you have my confidence as you already know. You have entrusted me with so many incident reports and I have assisted several times with proofreading. I am willing to assist you again," I calmly assure him as I finish getting dressed.

I sit down at my desk, grab a pen, and open the file folder. I am shocked to say the least at seeing such bloody photographs of the crew quarters. I look up at Amit with eyes wide even before reading the report.

"It's okay, Lincee, the men are in the Medical Centre getting treated and security personnel are in there with the Doctor." Amit reassures me to proceed.

I buckle down and read the report, making grammatical corrections with my pen. I am very disturbed as I read and can understand how difficult it must have been for Amit to write it. I finish reading the report as Amit gets dressed. I close the file folder and give Amit a quick kiss. Amit takes the folder and heads to the security office to edit the report and complete it for SECO to read at 9:00 a.m.

I am already shuddering at those images in the photographs. I have never seen so much blood, and then to have put in my mind the events and the entire story. I naturally am somewhat disturbed. Later in the day, after Amit gets a good sleep in his own cabin and I come back from exploring ashore, we meet in my cabin. I learn the two drunken sailors are still in the Medical Centre recovering and SECO has forwarded the incident report to the Captain who has forwarded it to Head Office with his decision. The two crew members will be terminated from the company and sent home as soon as they recover and are in a condition to travel back to the Philippines. Each of these crew members will disembark alone; they will not go home from the same port or take the same flight to ensure they do not continue their brawl off the ship. A security personnel member is stationed in the Medical Centre to ensure the safety of the medical team and to keep these two sailors from continuing to engage in their differences.

As soon the Senior Doctor announces that the attacking crew member is fit to be disembarked, security escorts him to his cabin; he has thirty minutes to pack up his personal effects before being escorted down the gangway. The port agent greets him at the bottom of the gangway as the officer from the Crew Office hands over his passport and flight itinerary. The Medical Department and Security Department breathe a sigh of relief as the man is now off the ship. Unfortunately, there is no other consequence that can be handed over to this crew member who attacked another fellow crew member. Was it attempted murder? Was it just assault, even when the stabbing was repeated? What else can the Captain do? What else can Head Office do? Other than to dismiss the employee from the company, not much else can be done to follow up on such behaviour. Such lawlessness exists at sea on international waters. No country wants to deal with crime on a cruise ship. No one wants to take responsibility for what happens on a cruise ship. Moreover, no one on land will ever know what this sailor did or what he is capable of other than what he himself reveals.

The injured sailor is still laying in the medical ward with his neck bandaged up. After a few days pass, this sailor wants to go home. The Senior Doctor reports to the Captain that the injured sailor is fit enough to disembark and travel. SECO determines that he does not require a security escort to his cabin as he is the victim of the assault. However, he too is dismissed from the company for unruly conduct and being inebriated. Many of the crew living in that crew corridor along Deck Two are still shaken by the incident; the bloody stains have been cleaned up but the memories and images haunt many of the crew members. I am relieved to hear that this sailor has recovered and is fit to be discharged and travel independently. Reading that incident report and seeing the crime pictures of these two sailors' brawl still haunt me to this day. I have never seen so much blood in my entire life nor do I ever want to see or read such a report ever again.

Chapter 11

Christmas in South Pacific

I wanted freedom, open air, adventure. I found it on the sea.
Alain Gerbault

wake up to the thundering sound of the anchor dropping, a sound that vibrates throughout the entire ship of 670 passengers off the coast of Bora Bora. This morning I lay in bed enjoying the comforts of my officer cabin under my blankets, thinking to myself that I am so blessed to be back at sea for another contract touring the islands of the South Pacific. When I returned home from my last contract touring the Mediterranean, I again had a hard time adjusting to life on land and the mundane routine of teaching clients at the gym. My mind and heart longed to be at sea with my boyfriend, Amit, even though I knew I would not see him again for quite some time; in fact, I wondered if our paths would ever cross again at sea. After a few months of working on land, I wholeheartedly accepted another contract to work the South Pacific entertaining passengers. A new opportunity, a new chapter, a new itinerary, and despite having no Amit to start this contract, I am so excited to explore a new part of the world.

Every day when the ship arrives into a port of call in French Polynesia, our ship drops anchor about three miles away from shore due to the shallow waters. Tender boats are lowered to usher the passengers to the mainland from our ship. The humid air always makes for a hot day ahead. Without even a hint of a breeze, you can smell the fresh, crisp, and unpolluted air as you gaze to the clear blue sky. What paradise on earth surrounds me every day and everywhere I look! The lush mountains and densely populated coconut trees dotting the atolls are a sight to behold. Each island we visit is unspoiled, and nature appears to be untouched, preserved, and protected. Not only is there an ambiance of peace, there is a sense of beauty to behold that the Mighty Creator has left His fingerprints everywhere you look. The wonder envelopes you as it takes your breath away; you can marvel in such glory with every step you take while exploring each South Pacific island.

As I stroll along the dirt road looking at the land crabs scurrying into their holes, I imagine myself retiring here on this remote island of Bora Bora. Life here is so peaceful, quiet, and simple in comparison to my hectic life back home in the big city. I would greatly appreciate coming here to escape, but I think after a while I would become bored and really miss my comforts, such as Starbucks. I wander into the local market to appreciate the native crafts and souvenirs available for sale. I look for a postcard even though I know it is highly unlikely that I will find one here. My eyes scan for a shot glass to add to my collection but to no avail. I end up taking some pictures of my surroundings and head back to the pier to catch the next tender boat back to the ship.

I get back to the ship with about four hours left to spare before my next shift. I could have stayed on Bora Bora for a bit longer, but I had already toured the entire island in two hours and had seen everything. Our ship will be back here in another twelve days, so I figure I can go for a snorkel with the stingrays when I return. For now, I just want a shower, eat a snack, and play some piano before my shift this evening.

Now I sit at the piano in the lounge on the top deck aft of the ship where I have an aerial view of the entire island of Bora Bora. What paradise it is for a pianist like me to be able to play with such a breathtaking view. The entire lounge is empty as all the passengers are ashore which gives me some private, quiet time to practice. In this lounge, I have some company as two bartenders are setting up the latest delivery.

I pull out my sheet music and warm up my hands before my fingers effortlessly glide over the keys. I warm up my vocal cords as my hands play some chords and scales. Within a few minutes, my voice is ready to belt out some of my favourite tunes. Such elation and glorious pleasure run through my being when I am at the piano singing my heart out. I don't even notice my surroundings or that the bar tenders have stopped working and are staring at me. After a few melodies, I stop to shuffle my music sheets to arrange them for another medley, and I look up to see one of the bartenders looking at me. I smile back and call across the lounge, "Was that tune good?"

Suddenly my pager goes off. I look at the number and it's coming from the Cruise Director's office. I walk over to the bar and ask to use the telephone. I call the Cruise Director who requests my presence for an unexpected and unscheduled meeting. After I hang up the telephone, the bartender and I exchange pleasantries. My practice time has just been cut short and now I must head all the way down to Deck Three on the other end of the ship to meet with the boss. I am not pleased as I pack up my music folder. I wonder what in the world she wants with me now. I hope whatever it is, it won't take long. I barely warmed up on the piano and I still have a lot of music in me to get out.

I walk into the Cruise Director's office to find her sitting at her desk with a concerned look on her face. "Thanks for coming on such short notice, Lincee. I called you here because I need some help and I'm hoping you can be the one to assist in my dilemma."

"Sure, I will help if I am able. What is it you need from me?" I reply in earnest.

The Cruise Director looks across her desk intently at me as I sit across from her. "Head Office just sent an email that they will not be sending a clergy member to deliver the Christmas Catholic or Protestant services. I have asked everyone in the Entertainment Department and the Bridge Officers and Captain and no one is able to deliver the Christmas services. I myself don't feel comfortable delivering such services for the passengers. Can you assist in any way?"

I pause as I look at her and think to myself, "Here we go again!" Then I answer, "Of course, I would be glad to be of assistance. What do you need? For me to play the piano?" I asked politely.

"No, Lincee, I need someone to prepare, plan, organize, deliver the sermon, and conduct the entire one-hour service for both the Protestant and Catholic services on Christmas Eve and Christmas Day. This is a tall order and I do not even know where to start. Can you do all of it including playing the piano?" She looks pleadingly into my eyes with much desperation.

Apparently she has heard that I am a part of the Christian Seafarers Mission and I assist with the Christian services for the crew onboard this ship. On this tiny ship of 670 passengers and 300 crew, word gets around fast and everyone knows everyone else's business, so there is no hiding that I am an active member of the fellowship despite being onboard for only two weeks.

"Sure, I can be of assistance. Leave the entire program to me and we can meet again tomorrow morning to finalize it," I calmly reassure her.

She sits back in her chair and breathes a sigh of relief. "Thanks a million, Lincee. I look forward to hearing your sermon!"

I leave the Cruise Director's office and head back to my cabin. I sit at my desk and open my laptop. I have a file folder of sermons I have delivered on previous ships on other contracts, but I realized I have never delivered a Christmas sermon. Yikes! Christmas and Easter sermons are the hardest and toughest. They are the pillars of the faith, and it takes a highly trained and qualified ordained minister to deliver these big ones. I look at the time and calculate the time difference back to North America; it is the wrong time to call back home and ask my pastor for some advice. Who am I to deliver the Christmas sermon? Little measly me? These are such big shoes to fill with a heavy weight of responsibility. I bow my head and earnestly pray for wisdom. I have heard many Christmas sermons over the last thirty years. I know the story of Christmas and I know the message of Salvation. The seeds have been planted deep in my heart and mind. In this moment, I need wisdom to harvest the Word and deliver it clearly to the passengers on this ship.

After much time in prayer, I take out my Bible and notepad. I open a new file on my computer and label the file "Christmas Sermon and Program." I get right to work. Within two hours, I have completed the entire program, service order, music selection, and sermon outline. My brain feels fried and my head is swimming. I debate whether to send an email to my pastor back home. I decide not to as I know I will not have time to follow up before I have to deliver the service. After a late-night working, I go to the Cruise Director's office to complete some paperwork, check emails, and print off tomorrow's schedule. It is now past midnight and I am ready to fall asleep. As I lay in my bed, I have a hard time shutting my brain off as my mind wanders to the last Christmas church service I attended. Tomorrow is Friday and Sunday is right around the corner. Not only do I have the passenger service to deliver on Sunday for Christmas day, I also want to attend the crew Christmas service which starts at 11:30 p.m.

When the day comes, I am incredibly nervous on stage delivering the Christmas sermon, more so than when I perform on the piano. Nonetheless, everything goes surprisingly well despite my trepidation in delivering the big sermon in the main lounge to the passengers. I am surprised to see some of the Bridge Officers in the lounge on Christmas Eve and Christmas Day. I think I have gained newfound respect from the officers after they attended the services.

This newly-earned respect is confirmed the next day when I get a surprise invitation to visit the Bridge by the Captain. That day around 3:00 p.m., while in a meeting in the Cruise Director's office, my pager goes off. I ignore the beeping as the most important person is sitting right in front of me and nobody else should be interrupting my meeting at this time of day. The beeping continues. The Cruise Director pipes up slightly annoyed with the interruption, "Lincee, who is paging you?"

I look down at my pager, surprised to see the Captain's office number. "It's the Captain paging me," I sheepishly reply to my boss.

"What? The Captain is paging you? Why? I am your boss. I am the Cruise Director and we are in a meeting now. Nobody interrupts me," she replies adamantly. "What is the number? I will call the Captain back."

At this point, I am a bit nervous as to why the Captain would be paging me at this critical time of the day. The ship's anchor is just about to be pulled up from the island of Hiva Oa and the Cruise Director is holding a big meeting with me to discuss the entertainment program for the next few days.

"Hello, Captain, this is the CD calling you on behalf of Lincee. She is in a meeting with me at the present time. She cannot return your page. Why do you need her?"

Frankly, the Cruise Directors nosing into my business is a bone of contention with me. Why is it that she must know the reason why the Captain is paging me? She pauses for a long time as the Captain speaks to her.

"Well, Lincee is busy now and cannot come to the Bridge. I will send her up as soon as we are done here. No, she cannot come now. You will have to pull the anchor up without Lincee on the Bridge. Sorry," she calmly yet politely speaks into the phone.

After she hangs up the phone, my boss looks at me with wide eyes. "Lincee, the Captain apparently needs *you* on the Bridge for the ship to sail. Why does he need you to be present in order for the ship to sail? I don't get it."

I am shocked at her questions. "I don't know ma'am. Let's just proceed with our meeting and I will find out afterward."

She shuffles her papers and continues, "Lincee, for some reason he says he can't pull the anchor up and sail the ship without your presence on the Bridge. Are you a Bridge Officer on the side assisting the Pilot and Captain aside from your other entertaining duties?"

"I don't know why the Captain paged me. This is the first time I've been paged by the Bridge," I awkwardly reply to her.

She exasperatedly shakes her head. "Well, let's quickly finalize the program and you better get up on the Bridge before the Captain gets upset with me!"

Within ten minutes, I rush out the Cruise Director's office and rush upstairs to the Bridge. The anchor has just pulled up when I ring the doorbell to the Bridge. I look right into the closed-circuit camera (CCCTV) posted on the ceiling and wave as the Captain buzzes to let me in.

"Lincee, you are here!" The Captain grabs my hand and leads me to the center bridge control panel and starts to narrate his navigation of the ship out of the harbour of Hiva Oa. I stand silently and observe the Captain at work with all the Bridge Officers. I try hard to remain calm and not appear a nervous nilly when I see every officer glance at me every few seconds. "What in the world is going on?" I think to myself. "Why have I been summoned up to the Bridge for sail away? How in the world am I going to explain this one to my boss?" I notice the Captain giving me glances every few minutes with a smile. I don't know what to think of such behaviour as I am totally out of my element.

I see the Staff Captain standing beside the Pilot at the center of the control panel. On the other end of the Bridge wing, I watch the Senior First Officer, Senior Second Officer, and Third Officer looking at the computer screens. On my end stands the Captain and one of the cadets while the Pilot gives directions. The Captain is walking back and forth between the two groups while the two watchmen with binoculars stand silently with their noses up against the Bridge window. Once the ship starts to sail, this shift of Bridge Officers will finish at 4:00 p.m., and then the First Officer, Second Officer and Senior Third Officer will arrive. It is complete silence on the Bridge while the Pilot speaks and directs the Captain and officers. The cadet and I stand with wide eyes observing and soaking up everything that unfolds moment by moment.

I am mesmerized at the operations on the Bridge. Moreover, I am fascinated at the two watchmen standing up against the center of the Bridge window with binoculars. "What an amazing job," I think to myself. "Your whole entire shift is just staring out the window with binoculars! What a neat job to have to just stand all day and only look out the window." I wonder what they are looking for through their binoculars. It has been half an hour and they are still looking through them; every so often, they put the binoculars down, turn to smile at me, and then go back to gazing out the window. I so desperately want to walk over to the window and just stand beside the watchmen and ask, "What are you looking for through those binoculars? Mermaids? Whales? Icebergs?"

I want to tell them that I think they have an amazing, stress-free job, never having to deal with demanding passengers, never having to deal with stressed fellow crew members from other departments, able to work in silence, peace, and quiet, and have no paperwork to do. Furthermore, to be in the presence of officers and in such a pleasant work environment is a dream job on any ship. This watchman's position is now the most coveted position of employment on this ship by this woman! I would love to be in the presence of all these handsome officers all day just staring out the window. Sign me up! At this present time, I am the only woman on this Bridge and I quite like the attention already. I wonder to myself how many women get to come up to the Bridge personally invited by the Captain?

If a teacher ever tells you to stop looking out the window during class in order to pay attention to the lesson, you could always say to the teacher, "One day I will get a job just to look out the window all day and get paid to do it!" I think back to all the times I sat in class and stared out the window daydreaming instead of concentrating on the lesson at hand. If only I knew such a job existed! The only downside of being a Bridge watchman is that your cabin is below deck, which is below the waterline, and you eat the in the Crew Mess. Your rank is still considered the lowest of the three ranks as crew status which means no privileges at all.

Instead of giving into my desire to walk around and talk to the watchmen at the window, I resolve to stand where I am told by the Captain and remain obedient rather than roam the Bridge and distract the officers by asking questions. I am thoroughly enjoying this privileged invitation as my eyes dart back and forth at all the men in uniform. When a man puts on a white uniform with stripes on his shoulders, he suddenly appears incredibly handsome to me regardless of how many stripes determine his rank. Unexpectedly, I feel like I am a kid in a candy shop looking and gazing at all these handsome officers in action. My shoulders relax as I take deep breaths, soaking up every moment of this opportunity and not wanting it to end. I think to myself that I should have brought my camera to get some pictures but then quickly realize if I had brought my camera, I would not be welcome as I am not a tourist or passenger; I am crew. No pictures are permitted on the Bridge or of the Bridge.

Precisely at 4:00 p.m., the shift change occurs, and the new officers arrive on the Bridge. The Captain motions for me to follow him out of the Bridge and into his office. I feel like I am going to the Principal's office as I walk silently beside him feeling nervous. The Captain's office is just outside the Bridge and across from his cabin. I am getting to see things that no crew member is permitted to see, and my nervousness grows. The Captain motions for me to take a seat and then he sits across from me. He smiles and asks in his thick Italian accent and charm, "How are you, Lincee? Did you enjoy the Bridge visit?"

"Thank you, Captain, for the invitation. Yes, I have thoroughly enjoyed the visit to the Bridge," I reply happily.

"Well, tomorrow we arrive on the island of Nuka Hiva. Would you like to come up again to the Bridge for sail away?" he asks with a smile.

I politely reply, "Sir, what time is sail away? I have to work tomorrow at 5:00 p.m.," as I try to recall the schedule for tomorrow.

"Well, tomorrow we sail at 5:00 p.m., so come to the Bridge at 4:30 p.m. Change your schedule start time," he tells me.

"Sir, I would like to come at 4:30 p.m. but I cannot as I will be preparing for my five o'clock shift," I explain.

"Are you not the boss in your department? Change the schedule. See you here tomorrow at 4:30 p.m., Lincee. I look forward to chatting with you again."

"Yes sir, I will do as you ask. Thank you for the invitation, Captain." I start to stand up, but the Captain is still sitting so I slowly sit back down and wait for him to stand first. He does not budge from his office chair.

"So, Lincee, how are you enjoying my ship so far? How is the contract coming along since you came onboard?" he asks me.

I enjoy the banter back and forth with the Captain, but it is now almost 5:00 p.m. as I check the clock hanging in his office and I am getting hungry. I really do not want this time to end but I really need to go eat and get ready for my 7:00 p.m. shift. I tell the Captain that my time is up, and I must go. We agree to meet tomorrow at 4:30 p.m. again in his office to chat prior to going onto the Bridge for sail away from the island of Nuka Hiva.

As I head back down toward Deck four, I think that I will definitely enjoy this contract. My mind is a whirlwind because of the events that have unfolded within the last three hours. I have so much work ahead of me and I am so excited to be on this ship even without my boyfriend, and now I have a new friend, the most important person on the ship—the Captain!

After leaving the Captains office, I walk along the i95 on Deck Four toward my cabin, which means I will pass the Medical Centre located in the center of the ship. I see a fellow crew member a few steps ahead of me wheeling his cleaning cart and dragging his vacuum cleaner towards the Medical Centre for his shift. I can see his hands are full, and he is trying to open the door with his key, so I jump in and offer to open and hold the door for him. He looks up and beams with a smile when he sees this officer offer a kind gesture and lend a helping hand. He pulls in the cleaning cart and I grab the vacuum cleaner and pull it inside the waiting room. Every day the cleaner comes in during the two-hour break that the Medical Centre is closed to the crew and passengers so a thorough cleaning can be done without interruption. The crew entrance is from the side of the i95 corridor and the passenger entrance is on the other side, and there are separate waiting rooms on either side of the reception desk, so passengers never see the crew members.

Between the two couches of the crew waiting room is a small table with a clipboard for crew to sign in and a bowl filled with free condoms. I can assure you; this bowl of free condoms is not available in the passenger waiting room.

As I hand over the vacuum cleaner to the fellow crew member, he tells me, "Thank you for your help, Lincee."

"No problem, anytime," I reply. I continue to look at him and I do not move.

He sees that I do not leave the Medical Centre and is bewildered. "Ms. Lincee, the Medical Centre is closed. You cannot stay here with me to clean."

"I know it's closed." I look down at the condom bowl and lean over to grab a few and stuff them in my pockets.

He stands holding the vacuum cleaner and smiles at me, so I continue to grab a few more and stuff them in my back pockets.

"Uumm, Ms. Lincee, you do know that the bowl is replenished every day. Do you really need that many for tonight?" he asks me with a big grin and wide, laughing eyes.

"It's not for me." I don't even look up as I reply, continuing to grab more condoms as I further explain, "Well, I don't want to have to come in here every time during office hours to take some and have everyone in the waiting room watch me." At this point, both my front and back pockets are full of condoms, so I decide to pick up the entire bowl and empty all the prophylactics into my shoulder bag. I gently place the empty bowl back onto the table between the couches.

The cleaner looks at me with such shock but keeps smiling and says not another word. I am sure he is in much disbelief as to what he has just witnessed. As I head out the Medical Centre, I tell him, "Thanks and...uummm...you never saw what just happened! Now I don't have to come back here for a while."

I empty my pockets and stuff all the condoms into my shoulder bag as I walk along the i95 corridor because I do not want to draw any attention or have any condoms falling out of my pockets. With about forty condoms in my purse, I now have the most coveted contraband on this ship in my possession. I can use it to my advantage and trade it for something of better value. Time to be Robin Hood and help those in need of a condom or two. I am excited to see how many I can trade away. Perhaps tonight I can get a few telephone cards in exchange for a few condoms or a few bottles of water. Time will tell how quickly I will offload all these condoms as I know I certainly will not have any use for this contraband since my boyfriend is not with me on this contract. I am now the condom dealer joining the underground black market, a title I never thought would be added to my description.

Chapter 12

Fire! Fire!

I need the sea because it teaches me.
Pablo Neruda

It is another glorious day to wake up to the comforts of my officer cabin on a king-sized bed. I feel like I am in a lap of luxury since I do not have a king-sized bed back home on land. I lay in bed this morning stretching as I look out my window with the Egyptian sunrise gleaming into my cabin. Today we docked in Port Said. I still cannot believe that I took on another three-month contract coming back across the Atlantic Ocean. Life back on land is now a distant memory and I cannot imagine going back to my boring, mundane routine. After my last contract sailing in the South Pacific, I once more had a hard time adjusting back to life on land instructing clients on how to reach their fitness goals in the gym. For six months, I felt restless and the sailor's blood was still coursing through my veins. Therefore, I wholeheartedly accepted another contract.

Life is a bit more exciting at sea because I feel pampered. Every day, I have someone who makes my bed, tends to my needs, and takes my laundry for service. My food is prepared and I can just get up and walk away from the dining table without a care to follow up, do the dishes, or grocery shop. Here at sea, I have the respect of all the heads of departments and officers in every zone on every deck of the ship. Anything I request or ask of for my own Entertainment Department is consistently met with respect and excellent service in a timely manner. In my work experience, I am unable to think of any position on land whereby this type of life is paralleled in any industry. Life as an officer at sea is very good.

The ship docked in Port Said at 5:00 a.m. The passengers started disembarking at 6:00 a.m. for their tour to see the Pyramids. This twelve-hour tour starts with a three-hour drive from Port Said to Cairo and another three-hour drive back from Cairo to Port Said. Spending six hours on a bus is not ideal, but the long, arduous journey is worth the drive to see the Pyramids. This week the Shore Excursion department has arranged the exact same tour for the crew and being on a bus for six hours with fellow crew members is like going on a school field trip. You are on an adventure with all your friends, laughing, singing, and talking to everyone because we all serve the same passengers and have a lot of notes to compare. This crew tour into the heart of Cairo involved several directives from the Captain and the Doctor, and tours do not normally involve senior officers.

Every week, when the passengers come back from this exact same tour, they vomit and have diarrhea for the remainder of the cruise. During the tour, the passengers often stop at the Kentucky Fried Chicken fast food restaurant across from the Pyramids, drink local beverages with ice cubes, and then vomit and have diarrhea so bad that the entire ship is put on a severe, high-alert, red-level sanitation to prevent a norovirus outbreak.

This week the Doctor informs the Captain that he cannot afford to have all the crew members come back from the Pyramids vomiting and having diarrhea as the passengers have done so on the previous cruises. If this should happen, it will mean that the crew would need to be quarantined for three days, resulting in every department being short crew members. That many sick crew members would be a disaster for the medical team to deal with on top of the already ill passengers in quarantine. Therefore, the Doctor and Captain devise a plan to ensure that every crew member is given a large, packed lunch to eat during the bus tour.

On this morning of the tour, the crew members are assembled at 5:00 a.m. in the Crew Bar for instructions prior to disembarking the ship. Each of us are given our passports and our visas to go ashore as Egyptian immigration officials are present and waiting to stamp our paperwork as we cross the gangway. After the ninety of us are given our passports, the lunch bags that the Head Chef of the galley prepared are distributed. We pick up our bag after we sign our names on a paper that we each received a lunch. Each contains a balanced meal to last the entire day. I see a sandwich wrapped in plastic wrap, a large bottle of water, a banana, an apple, a cookie, and a chocolate bar. The Doctor makes one final announcement before we leave the Crew Bar.

"Please DO NOT eat any food from the Kentucky Fried Chicken in Egypt. Do not eat any food from vendors and only drink bottled water. I expect all of you back to work when you return and nobody to be ill in my Medical Centre. Is that understood?"

All the crew murmur a tired "Yes, Doctor," as the clock approaches 5:45 a.m.

Then the Doctor continues, "Lincee here is the officer on the bus. She will remind you and watch over you as to not to eat at KFC. Have a great time at the Pyramids. Come back all safe and sound."

I am shocked hearing the last few words of the Doctor. What? I am now in charge of this bus tour? Nobody consulted me on this responsibility. This is news to me so early in the morning. I am to make sure my fellow crew members behave according to the Doctor's wishes? I must babysit my fellow crew members? Did I hear that correctly? I comment to myself, "Hhhmmm, I don't think so!" Surely, I am not going to tell my fellow crew members how to conduct themselves ashore. There are ninety crew members going on this tour; two full buses which comprise almost one-third of the entire crew onboard this ship. These people are all adults in their respective departments. They can be responsible enough to represent the company in their own conduct, character, and conversation. I will not babysit my fellow crew members. I am on tour to make memories and have a good time too.

As the bus pulls away from Port Said, the crew members chat away but, within thirty minutes, they are all fast asleep.

Many of the crew finished their shift last night around midnight and some of the casino staff finished work at 3:00 a.m. this morning. So, to be up for a 5:00 a.m. meeting for disembarkation instructions is a toll on the body for any sailor in any department. Everyone is fast asleep to be well-rested for the arrival in Cairo in about two hours. I am wide awake, enjoying looking out the window to take in all that Egypt has to offer. I am fascinated to see the infrastructure, the architectural designs of the buildings, and the local people hustling and bustling about to start their day. I surely do not want to sleep and miss a single moment of my journey into Cairo. This is my third time on this crew bus tour. I had the privilege of doing this tour twice in my previous Mediterranean contract with my Amit, so I have already made some wonderful memories in Egypt with him.

Around 8:00 a.m., the crew start to wake up as the bus goes through morning traffic in Cairo, and the excitement builds as we approach the heart of the city. Everyone wakes up hungry and quickly devours the contents of their packed lunch, chatting and enjoying the view in the air-conditioned comfort of the bus. Almost everyone has demolished the contents of the lunch bag provided by the company. I pull out the large, plastic garbage bag and start to walk up and down the bus to collect all the paper bags, banana peels, apple cores, and chocolate wrappers. I am dismayed to see that the crew have already filled the garbage bag which means that by twelve noon, they will be hungry again as they wander around the Pyramids. I can already foresee the crew members drooling for a soda pop and the comforts of greasy food such as Kentucky Fried Chicken. Crew food on the ship becomes bland and boring after the first two weeks at sea, so any type of food on land is considered comfort food, to say the least.

As the bus rounds the corner, the splendor of the monumental Pyramids is revealed as the bus slowly moves with traffic along the 5 km road leading up the ancient wonders. The excitement, ooooohs and ahhhhhs, and squeals of the crew remind me of excited children on a school bus trip. Cameras and phones are whipped out as the crew feverishly snap pictures through the large bus windows. The bus driver, tour guide, bodyguard, and I have exchanged pleasantries throughout the three-hour drive into Cairo from Port Said. I notice that none of these Egyptian people have a packed lunch. I have been given extra rations of food by the Doctor and decide to share it with each of them; they graciously accept my offer of food.

As the bus parks by the Pyramids, the tour guide stands up to make announcements as the bodyguard steps down from the bus with his Zastava M21 assault rifle strapped across his chest. After the tour guide speaks, I stand up to speak and finish off with the Doctor's reminder. The eager crew anticipating getting off the bus respond to me with boos; "Lincee, you are one of us! Let us have fun!" I smile as I get off the bus first right on the heels of the tour guide. Around lunch time, I turn a blind eye when I see a flock of crew lining up at the Kentucky Fried Chicken in a line that stretches out the front door and down the sidewalk. Personally, I had packed an extra bottle of water and extra food in my backpack. I surely don't want to be ill from tasting food on land.

As a crew member, I have witnessed enough sick fellow crew members and passengers who delved into food on land only to come back to the ship and put in quarantine suffering extreme discomfort and pain for several days. As the head of my department, I am extremely prudent as I know I cannot afford to be ill as I have a team of people to look after. I walk past the long line of people standing outside the door of the fast food restaurant as the crew jokingly shout at me, "You don't see us, Lincee! We don't see you, Lincee!" I turn a blind eye as I continue exploring on my own.

I walk along the sidewalk taking in the sights and sounds of Cairo. I am fascinated to see in a back alley between businesses a posse of camels standing in the shade alongside a bunch of chickens running loose. Back home in North America, in the back alleys, I normally see trash and recycling bins and perhaps a rat, yet here in Cairo I see camels and chickens. Immediately, I think to myself that these must be the chickens they use for the Kentucky Fried Chicken restaurant. With wide eyes, I cannot stop looking between the wild chickens running about between the legs of the camels and back behind me to the long line of people leading up to the doorsteps of KFC. I shake my head and keep walking up the sidewalk.

It is twelve noon and the streets of Cairo are bustling with traffic. On the road, less than two feet from me, I see people in cars stuck in traffic, hand-pulled rickshaws, and carriages pulled by horses all in one lane. I see people on motorcycles and camels in the same lane of traffic too. In the other lane, heading the opposite direction, I see the same type of traffic lined up behind one another. Animals and vehicles in the same lane just boggle my mind. The aromas surrounding me are an assault on the senses. I hear constant cars honking, camel and horse noises, and engines of motorcycles roaring all at the same time as I stroll along mesmerized at my surroundings. The constant cacophony of noise pollution is simply unbelievable to my North American ears.

After the long, three-hour drive back into Port Said from Cairo, our bus pulls onto the pier where our ship is docked, and the tired crew slowly wakes up from the ride. So far it has been a whirlwind of a day of everyone making memories. It is now 6:00 p.m. and duty calls as it is time to board the ship, return our passports to the Crew Office, wash up, eat dinner, and be ready to serve the passengers by 6:30 p.m. with a smile on our faces. Each of us have been up since 5:00 a.m. and now we are expected to be ready, alert, and provide excellent, friendly service to the passengers regardless of how we feel.

The music starts up in the atrium and lounges, the venues are filled with entertainment, and the dining rooms are filled with passengers. The clock strikes 7:30 p.m. and every passenger goes about their vacation as the crew work tirelessly. The ship left Port Said half an hour ago at 7:00 p.m. Suddenly, the crew alert signal is sounded. The bells on the ship ring seven short blasts and one long blast. The crew immediately stop all service and walk quickly and quietly to the crew exits, return to their cabins to retrieve their life jackets, and report to muster stations. The passengers around the ship are left alone in the passenger areas. It is an eerie scene on a ship when one does not see a single crew member in sight. The passengers are fully aware that something is definitely amiss when the crew disappear. Within a few minutes, the Captain makes an announcement for all passengers to return to their cabins to retrieve to their life-jackets and immediately go to their muster stations.

Then the Captain makes an announcement in the crew quarters so that the passengers do not hear the nature of the emergency. "BRAVO, BRAVO, BRAVO. Attention all crew! Attention all crew! Assessment Party, Deck Two, Engine Room. I repeat, Assessment Party, Deck Two, Engine Room. BRAVO, BRAVO, BRAVO!"

The call signals that an engine has blown up and an extremely large and dangerous fire is in session. The fire is so fierce that the Assessment Party steps back for the firemen to take over. A fire at sea is the worst kind of peril to experience right next to the ship sinking. Our ship left the pier about thirty minutes ago and surely if we needed assistance, the Captain would have radioed for shoreside aid from the Egyptian authorities.

This engine fire is at the beginning stage, but it can get much worse very quickly and completely blow up the entire back half of the ship within a short period of time if it's not contained. All the crew are in place and stationed in their positions as the passengers slowly saunter to their muster station not realizing the severity of the situation. The crew is informed by radio that we will have to move all the passengers to the front of the ship as the engine room is located near the back of the ship and could blow up. The fumes and heat start to rise up to the passenger Deck Four and everyone looks worried as we move the passengers away from the fumes.

As an officer, I am in charge of mustering the group of passengers in my station. I have a lifeboat already assigned to my department, so I am not worried that I will die or be swimming in the cold, Egyptian water. However, I am getting worried that we may not get to the lifeboat in time before the ship blows up. The Captain announces that since all the passengers and crew members are at the front of the ship, only the lifeboats in the front of the ship will be lowered. This means we are now short six lifeboats. Some people will not get off this ship and onto a saving boat, and that includes my lifeboat because it is located at the stern of the ship. Only lifeboats in the bow will be lowered. My mind screams, "Crap! I just might die today! Today is the day I might perish at sea." I remind myself to take deep breaths and remain calm. I am an officer in charge and must lead. But God forbid if we find ourselves swimming in the waters just off the coast of Port Said. Then there is no rank or status and the uniform no longer exists; it is each to their own. I certainly will not take care of any passenger at that point.

The Captain radios us officers to inform us that Egyptian shoreside marine assistance is bringing us to shore due to the lifeboat shortage. One officer comes up to me and quietly relays another piece of information. "Whatever you do Lincee, DO NOT get into an Egyptian lifeboat. Stay with the crew and only board the ship's lifeboats okay? You do not want to disappear into thin air on an Egyptian lifeboat with the passengers. Who knows where you will be taken to in this dark night? And there is no accountability either. Stick with the company lifeboat and only assist passengers into the other lifeboats." She pauses and then continues, "Lincee, do you understand me? I repeat only *assist* the passengers onto the lifeboats. The crew will leave last in our own company lifeboat." I nod in acknowledgement with wide eyes as she walks away.

In my heart, I start to panic. What if the engine blows up the entire back of the ship? I won't have time to load the passengers and then find a crew lifeboat for myself. I decide if that happens, I will jump overboard to keep from burning alive. As I stand on deck calmly directing passengers, I see little boats with lights approaching the ship in the pitch-dark night even though it is only 8:30 p.m. These must be the Egyptian boats sent to assist us during this perilous time. I keep a constant look out for my fellow officers to ensure I am not forgotten or left behind with no crew lifeboat. Perhaps today is the day I die; I never thought such a day would come, yet I have always been mentally prepared to die at sea.

As sailors working in the cruise industry, we know that danger lurks onboard and that there is always the slim possibility of dying at sea despite all the advanced technology today on a luxury cruise ship. The rough seas can turn disastrous without a moment's notice, a virus can break out, a steel bollard can fly into the ship and sink it, or an engine can blow up like today. Anything can happen and it's always at the most unexpected time that such events unfold, many unbeknownst to the vacationing passenger. The crew is always aware of the severity of the emergency and is trained not to alarm the passengers, yet in my heart I realize that today may be the day I perish at sea and I don't even have my boyfriend onboard this ship to die with me. I will go down into the Egyptian waters alone.

"God help me!" I cry out as the thick smoke trails up to Deck Five. The engine fire is blazing, and the smoke is so thick that I start to cough. Passengers all around are coughing, covering their mouths and noses with their hands or sleeves. Every crew member knows that as long as we are on the ship and in uniform, we remain on duty representing the company. Once again in my life, images of the *Titanic* flash before my eyes as I see the panicked looks of the passengers' faces surrounding me as they board the lifeboats.

I wake up the next day in my king-sized bed in the comforts of my private cabin. I am delighted to be back in the safety of my crew quarters. This morning, Head Office sent a team of people directly to our ship in order to help the passengers rebook their flights, assist in their disembarking, and making sure they have a smooth transition to the airport for their connections safely back to their respective countries.

Last night, the Egyptian government sent enough assistance to keep the ship afloat and the fire was put out by the exhausted crew after a grueling few hours that passed beyond midnight. So much damage had spread throughout the ship that it could not sail and therefore had to be tugged back to Port Said by the Egyptian marine unit. Within twenty-four hours, all the passengers are offloaded and on their way home. The three hundred crew remain on the ship while Head Office tries to sort out the details and figure out how to repair the damaged ship. I am so glad to be alive today. I did not die in the waters of Egypt! I am not quite ready to meet my Creator as I believe I still have some work left to accomplish here on earth.

The passengers all disembarked the sixth day of this twelve-day cruise, so the Provision Master has plenty of food for the remainder of the cruise; the perishable food needs to be consumed before it goes bad. Happily, the crew get to consume the same food as the passengers without the passengers being present onboard. The quality and quantity of food increases wonderfully for the remaining crew on the ship.

Many of my fellow crew members are emotionally and mentally drained, and some are even traumatized by the ordeal and events that have unfolded over the last forty-eight hours. Without the passengers onboard, we are left to deal with our own thoughts, which of course leads us to find ways to pass the time and deal with the residual effects of such stress. Cheap alcohol, cigarettes, and sex are often a sailor's comfort and temporary escape from reality when stuck at sea.

Each crew member is apportioned a specific ration of pleasures dictated by Head Office. Every two weeks, the ship holds a sale called Cambusa for the crew. Each crew member is limited to purchase two bottles of alcohol, a carton of cigarettes, and one case of water every two weeks from the ship's Provision Master. Every purchase by a crew member is swiped and recorded by his or her crew card so as to ensure that no person over-consumes and becomes inebriated. I am pleased with the Cambusa prices. Now, a case of 1.5L bottles of water that contains ten bottles costs $8 USD. It is a good savings and a great convenience. Usually one can purchase individual bottles of 1.5L for $1 USD in the Crew Bar which is only open from 11:00 p.m. to 1:00 a.m.

On my officer account, I only purchase cases of water every two weeks. Every day I drink a 1.5L of bottled water on top of the cranberry juice, orange juice, and milkshakes whenever I can get them at sea. For the past ten years at sea, I have never purchased any alcohol or cigarettes on my officer account. I am known as the water girl and proud to have a healthy diet. Since growing up in a gym environment and working in the community gym all my life, I have learned to exercise self-control and manage my food and liquid intake.

One day at the gym, when I was seventeen years old, a bodybuilder saw me drink a can of Coca-Cola with a beef patty in my other hand. He came up to me and gently said, "Lincee, may I share a few words of wisdom with you?" He continued, "Please do take care of your body. Only you can decide what to put into your body. Be sure it has nutritional value." That point stuck in my mind and heart that one person would care enough about me to give me such a precious nugget of wisdom. Since that day forward, I have not touched another carbonated soda drink and have never put any form of alcohol into my body.

People often ask me why I do not drink alcohol or how I deal with stress that comes along life's journey without the aid of liquor. I always answer back, "Alcohol is only a temporary, band-aid solution to escape one's own reality at the cost of one's health. I prefer not to poison my body. If I need to take my body and mind for a spin, I exercise or do my Music. At sea, both are my saving Grace. And if I do not like my circumstances, I don't escape with poison; I face my circumstances head-on or change my situation." This reply often leaves them pondering.

Well today, my neighbour on the other side of my cabin comes knocking at my door. "Lincee, I noticed that since you joined the ship, you only purchase cases of water during Cambusa. Can you do me a favour?" he asks in his thick Macedonian accent.

"Sure, what can I do for you?" I reply smiling.

He willingly offers me this proposal. "Can you put some purchases on your account for me and I can purchase a case of water on my account for you? I will even deliver the heavy case of water to your door since we are neighbours and I will pay you in cash the difference."

"Okay, what would you like to purchase on my account?" I ask already knowing he wants alcohol and cigarettes.

"I want a bottle of Jack Daniels, Johnnie Walker, and a carton of cigarettes," he smiles back.

"You do know that by me doing this favour for you, I am enabling you to over consume your allotted weekly allowance, right?" I reply with raised eyebrows.

He smiles and jokingly replies back to me, "You do know that by me doing this favour for you, I am enabling you to over consume your allotted weekly allowance of water, right?"

I laugh at his response to me. No one has ever said such words to me, and to hear my own words thrown back into my face just tickles my fancy enough that I am willing to purchase Johnnie Walker and Jack Daniels for him every two weeks on my account. In my mind, it is a fair exchange for my fellow crew member to deliver the heavy case of water directly to my cabin.

Cambusa day arrives two days later and my neighbour eagerly knocks on my door. We walk together along the i95 corridor on Deck Four then down to Deck Two to the lengthy line of crew members eagerly anticipating their bi-weekly rations. We have discussed how we will proceed with the additional purchases on our accounts so as to not raise any suspicion. When I step up to the counter, I slide across my crew card along with my order requesting the following items: one case of water, one Johnnie Walker, one Jack Daniels, and one large carton of 200 cigarettes.

Antonio looks up at me with raised eyebrows, "Hello, Ms. Lincee, um, is this your order today?"

"Yes sir, as you see it," I reply without any hesitation.

"Ms. Lincee, what has happened to you? Did the stress of the fire push you over the edge? You have such poison on this request, I don't understand. What happened? Perhaps it's time to disembark?" Antonio asks with sincere concern.

The fellow crew members in line behind me overhear this long conversation and are surprised to hear Antonio pepper me with such questions. I just smile back, "Yes, Antonio, that is my order for today."

Antonio brings to the counter a case of water, Jack Daniels, Johnny Walker, and a carton of cigarettes. He motions the delivery boy to assist in delivering the heavy case of water for me. I grab each bottle of alcohol and tuck the carton of cigarettes under my arm as I leave.

As I walk past the long line of crew members, every single sailor looks at me wide eyed and taunts me with comments. All are surprised to see me with such rations in my arms. Some crew member jokes, "Yo, Lincee is now a REAL sailor!" Another chides in, "Lincee has gone mad!"

"Lincee, you need some sex to go with that order?"

"Lincee, I am available to come to your cabin if you want company with Johnny and Jack."

"Lincee has gone over the edge!"

"Lincee, what happened to you?"

"Lincee, what did the passengers do to you to make you turn to such poison?"

"Lincee, do you want some help putting out your fire?"

"Lincee, wanna ride me with Johnnie and Jack?"

"Look out! It's sailor Lincee!"

I have never heard so many comments in my life directed at me from a line of men standing for Cambusa.

I just hold my head up and smile as I walked back up to Deck Five towards my cabin. Once I reached the door of my cabin, my neighbour comes up behind me and drops a case of water and takes the Johnny Walker, Jack Daniels, and carton of cigarettes.

"What a fantastic trade!" he beams at me with a wide smile. "Thanks for all your help."

"I think my reputation is now tarnished and I just did the walk of shame from Deck Two Cambusa to my cabin," I reply sheepishly while shaking my head.

"No harm done, Lincee; this is the sailor's life! Enjoy the company and adventure," my neighbour reassures me.

"Yeah, no harm done. No harm done," I reply, trying to reassure myself that a sailor's life is never tarnished. It is just another adventure of being a sailor at sea. Once the sea touches your soul, life on land is never the same. I will never look at Johnnie Walker, Jack Daniels, and cigarettes the same way ever again.

Acknowledgements

Thank you to all the passengers who choose to take a cruise as part of your vacation. Without you, there would be no cruise industry. Thank you for choosing to make memories alongside sailors at sea. No matter the ship, crew members always strive to serve you to the best of their abilities, even under circumstances they are unable to control, such as inclement weather. Thank you for your patience, kindness, and for most of all, for making the experiences at sea memorable for both yourselves and the crew.

Thank you to all the seafarers for your hard work, utmost dedication, and lessons you teach one another as you make memories at sea and ashore in the wonderful ports of call.

My deepest gratitude to John, Patricia, and M. Smith for reading this manuscript in its early stages and sharing thoughts and ideas to make it the finished product you hold in your hands.

For seeing the potential in this book and making it a reality, I would like to thank my wonderful team of professionals at Xulon Press who helped me put this book together, and my insightful editor for helping me make my story come alive on the page.

Thank you to my friends and family who stood alongside me through all my joys, trials, and tribulations over the years. And finally, to my mother who demonstrated an exemplary walk of faith that I witnessed from a young age. It instilled in me an unwavering and steadfast quality of resilience and fortitude I hold to this day.

My gratitude, most especially to God, is unbounded.

Sermon Notes:
GODS GIFTS versus OUR GIFTS

1) People share gifts
2) God's gift to humanity, John 3:16
3) Our gift to God. What is your gift to God?
4) Our earthly responsibility. Are you treating it as a Job or Ministry?

JOB or MINISTRY?

Some people have a JOB as a Christian and others involve themselves in a MINISTRY.

What is the difference?

Ministry	Job	Scripture
If you are doing it to serve the Lord, it is a MINISTRY.	If you are doing it just because no one else will, it is a JOB.	Romans 12:11 Never be lacking in zeal, but keep your spiritual fervor, serving the Lord.
If you keep on serving, it is a MINISTRY.	If you quit because no one else praised you, or thanked you, it was a JOB.	2 Chronicles 15:7 But as for you, be strong and do not give up, for your work will be rewarded.
If you are committed to staying with it even when it means letting go of other earthly things, it is a MINISTRY.	If you will do it only as long as it does not interfere with your other activities, it is a JOB.	Psalm 9:10 Those who know your name will trust in you, for you, Lord, have never forsaken those who seek you. Deuteronomy 31:6 Be strong and of good courage do not fear nor be afraid; for the Lord your God He is the One who goes with you. He will not leave you nor forsake you.
If you stay with it even though nobody recognizes your efforts, it is MINISTRY.	If you quit because no one else praised you, or thanked you, it was a JOB.	Psalm 37:4 Delight yourself in the Lord and he will give you the desires of your heart.

Ministry	Job	Scripture
It is almost impossible not to be excited about a MINISTRY.	It is hard to get excited about a JOB.	Deuteronomy 28:12 The Lord grant you abundant prosperity.
If our concern is faithfulness, it is a MINISTRY.	If our concern is success, it is a JOB.	Hebrews 10:23 Let us hold unswervingly to the hope we profess, for he who promised is faithful
A great and growing church is filled with people involved in MINISTRY.	An average church is filled with people doing JOBS.	John 17:4-5 I have brought you glory on earth by completing the work you gave me to do.
If you have a JOB, give it up and find a MINISTRY.	If GOD call you to a MINISTRY, don't treat it like a JOB.	Isaiah 46:11 From the east I summon a bird of prey; from a far-off land, a man to fulfill my purpose. What I have said, that will I bring about; what I have planned, that will I do.

Appendix 2

<u>Sermon notes:</u>
PATIENCE

1) What is Patience?
2) How does God teach us to be patient?
3) When do we get what we want?
4) When and how do our prayers get answered?

Matthew 7:7-8

"Ask and it will be given to you; seek and you will find; knock and the door will be opened to you. For everyone who asks receives; the one who seeks finds; and to the one who knocks, the door will be opened."

1	James 5:7-8	Be patient, then, brothers and sisters, until the Lord's coming. See how the farmer waits for the land to yield its valuable crop, patiently waiting for the autumn and spring rains. You too, be patient and stand firm, because the Lord's coming is near.
2	1 Peter 2:20	But how is it to your credit if you receive a beating for doing wrong and endure it? But if you suffer for doing good and you endure it, this is commendable before God.
3	Galatians 6:9	Let us not become weary in doing good, for at the proper time we will reap a harvest if we do not give up.
4	Hebrews 10:23	Let us hold unswervingly to the hope we profess, for he who promised is faithful.
5	Matthew 24:13	But the one who stands firm to the end will be saved.
6	Hebrews 6:12	We do not want you to become lazy, but to imitate those who through faith and patience inherit what has been promised.
7	Hebrews 10:36	You need to persevere so that when you have done the will of God, you will receive what he has promised.

8	James 1:2-4	Consider it pure joy, my brothers and sisters, whenever you face trials of many kinds, because you know that the testing of your faith produces perseverance. Let perseverance finish its work so that you may be mature and complete, not lacking anything.
9	Romans 5:3-4	Not only so, but we also glory in our sufferings, because we know that suffering produces perseverance; perseverance, character; and character, hope.
10	Psalm 1:1-3 **STAND, SIT, and WALK.**	Character- Conduct- Conversation. How do we behave as a child of GOD? Blessed is the one who does not walk in step with the wicked or stand in the way that sinners take or sit in the company of mockers. But whose delight is in the law of the Lord, and who meditates on his law day and night. That person is like a tree planted by streams of water, which yields its fruit in season and whose leaf does not wither – whatever they do prospers.

About the Author

As a sailor at sea,

I fell in love with the sight of the sunrises and sunsets.

I fell in love with the smell of the salt air.

I fell in love with the sound of the waves.

I fell in love with the feeling of excitement as we sailed to each port of call.

I fell in love with the thought of hope each day brings.

I fell in love with the opportunities to learn and explore.

I fell in love with putting on the uniform and being a part of a team.

I fell in love with meeting and entertaining people from all corners of the earth.

I fell in love with the routine and knowing the schedule to come.

I fell in love with the surroundings of decadence.

I fell in love with the awesome wonder of seeing miracles and happiness unfold each day for passengers and fellow crew members.

I fell in love with the sailor who captured my heart.

I fell in love with being a seafarer.

I fell in love with making awesome memories stored deep in my heart.

I fell in love with being excited for another contract at sea and the adventures that lay ahead.

The blood of a sailor now pumps daily in my being.

I fell in love with the faith that strengthened me to walk this journey.

Most of all, I fell in love with the Almighty Creator who put me here to enjoy the splendor of this journey.

About the Illustrator

*M*y passion for art and drawing is something that has been an innate part of my growing up in Colombia. Growing up as a kid, I would spend my time reading old comic books and trying to reproduce all the pictures that intrigued my mind and heart.

With every opportunity I had, I realized there was not a piece a paper that did not leave without an imprint of my doodling. With the writing utensil in my hand, my mind was satiated with the illustrations that would pour forth, and at times this was how my mental appetite managed to escape from my reality.

Working at sea enabled my talents to mature over the period of being a seafarer which has been a journey of excitement to unexpected tumultuous periods of solitude and loneliness. My illustrations depict the life of a crewmember and the many moments that capture the memories, experiences, resilience and fortitude that each individual encounters.

I look forward to further developing my artistic aptitude in various creative avenues while depicting stories in my illustrations from all walks of life around the world.

Author: L.C. Tang

Illustrator: Oscar David

Instagram: osc_david1

Facebook: L.C. Tang

Facebook: Crew
Member Illustrated

CPSIA information can be obtained
at www.ICGtesting.com
Printed in the USA
LVHW010002041022
729893LV00027B/522